Nan

Here's to
Getting it Right!

Get it Right Jack ...and Jane

Hayela

ISBN: 1451538057
EAN-13: 9781451538052

DATING

Get it Right Jack ...and Jane

Angela Grammatico & Susan Scheuer
Educators in the Art of Dating
www.Getitrightjackandjane.com

Table of Contents

Acknowledgments

We would like to thank all those who have inspired us with their wisdom, knowledge and their life experiences. Including those we have dated, who through their own different styles, taught us the "do's and don'ts" of the dating process and to Dr. Terry Lyles who believed in us and our message. A special thanks to our parents Joseph and Vita Grammatico and Robert and Beverly Scheuer who have always been there to support and love us throughout our life's journey. And, to everyone who has sat or stood behind a chair at the Palace Hair Salon, whose tales of life have dramatically inspired this book, thank you! Also, we thank the team of incredible people at All The World's A Stage, that work so diligently to help "at risk" kids and have helped us to recognize the good that can come of selflessly supporting those in need. Finally, to our dearest friends and family, who have been our greatest cheerleaders, we love you all. All of you have truly inspired us to recognize the tender side of life and the true connection of love that we share with everyone around us.

Foreword

*G*et it Right Jack . . . and Jane* is a must read for everyone single, married, or single again because all relationships require "regular dating" to explore the other person and even remain connected in a long term relationship. I have coached thousands of individuals and couples looking to find and maintain loving relationships and at the top of my list is dating on a regular basis. Singles need to know the rules for dating. *Get it Right Jack . . . and Jane* provides funny, down to earth, and practical insight to minimize the confusion and pain that dating can cause.

Couples need the same insight to maintain a healthy and vibrant loving relationship and the key to longevity with another person is keeping it fresh. Couples that are not winning their mates daily, run the increased risk of losing that special person to someone else who is willing to win them over that day. Living with the beginning in mind helps to maintain a real spark to any relationship that usually forgets the first "treats" of romancing that leads to potential love success.

I strongly recommend this articulate approach to dating as a must read for anyone dating, or needing to date in a long-term relationship, to be reminded of what Angela and Susan share as the best and worst ways to succeed at this very confusing maze of DATING!

Terry Lyles, Ph.D.
Stress and Crisis Expert
terrylyles.com

Introduction

It all began with a martini!

While sitting at the bar at a local pub, we noticed a table of men gawking at the women as they strolled by. Yet not one of these women noticed nor even glanced in their direction. While witnessing the same guys mopping up the drool left on the table, we looked at each other and said "those poor saps don't stand a chance with those women." As a humanitarian service, we decided we really needed to help them! That led to a discussion of our own more hilarious dating experiences over the years. We also discussed the stories of our friends and clients who have shared their experiences with us as well. It occurred to us, over the course of our years of dating, that men and women really do want to make a good impression on their dates, but fall short for various reasons. Hence, the birth of what we believe will be an informative guidebook for you single guys and gals looking to make good impressions.

Get it Right Jack and Jane, is designed to help guide you and ease your anxiety as you go through the initial step by step process of dating. People have told us that they just don't know what to do on a first date, much less, continuing on to a second date. In light of this, we believe that this dating guidebook should give you some common sense advice that will lead you to a successful dating experience and beyond. You will learn how to enjoy your dating experiences.

We have tailored this book to help you see where some of the most common pitfalls lay that may have tripped you up in the past. We will guide you in building your confidence, your knowledge, and recognizing your shortcomings so that you overcome any negative attitudes you've had about dating. We will provide you with the tools necessary to regain belief in yourself and your ability to meet and date successfully. With the correct tools, dating can be very easy and fun!

Now, we want to make it clear that we are not psychologists and this should not be considered a "relationship help" book. We are simply two single girls with more experience in the singles life than we might care to admit. We offer a dose of realistic and informative insight on: (1) how to get to and be successful on a first date; (2) how to watch out for those ten deadly sins; (3) why they don't call you back; (4) how to fill out an on-line dating profile; and (5) getting through the first three months of a relationship. Remember, you can't get to the second date, if you blow the first one!

While some men and women might be resistant in seeking help of this nature, we can assure you that if you give this guidebook a glance you just may find that it's much easier to follow than you think. It really does work! We are not suggesting that you cannot be creative in your own right on how to conduct your-self in the dating process; however, will you at least consider that we may be able to offer a few pointers and get you headed in the right direction? This dat-ing guidebook will help deter you from making a se-ries of blunders that could have been prevented. We are looking to get you on the right path to successful dating and more.

We were both young girls when artists like Diana Ross and The Supremes, Marvin Gaye, the Jackson 5, the Four Tops and the Temptations first hit the radio airwaves. It didn't take long for everyone to see that the Motown sound would change the music industry forever. As most of us Detroit natives know, Motown Records got its start in 1959, by founder Barry Gordy, in a house at 2648 West Grand Boulevard, Detroit, Michi-gan, fondly known as Hitsville USA. While Mr. Gordy eventually moved his recording studio to Los Angeles and closed operations in Detroit, many of us still be-lieve that the heart and soul of the Motown sound will forever remain a part of the Detroit culture.

Having both grown up in Motown, we feel a strong connection to the music that put Detroit on the map of the music industry. The rhythm of the music courses through our veins and we remember times when a certain favorite Motown song would come on the radio and everyone (young and old) in our households would stop what they were doing and start moving to the music. The Motown sound brings back many happy memories for us. As you continue to read, we hope you find our references to the various Motown hits throughout the book a way for you to connect with us on a more personal level. For some of you it may even bring a smile to your face as you reflect on your own memory of a time past. In the words of Martha and the Vandellas, "(Love is Like a) Heat Wave," so let's turn up the heat!

CHAPTER 1

Ain't No Mountain High Enough

You keep me Hanging On

"Hooking up" is a term used by the 20 some-things that refers to hanging out in groups and getting to know people before deciding to date. Hooking up can also refer to intimate encounters with "friends" that requires little or no emotional or relationship commitment. These "group dates" if you will, lend themselves to people sending a lot of mixed signals by being flirtatious and becoming intimate, but with no commitment to follow. For guys, hooking up does not allow them to do what comes naturally, which is pursuing the object of their desire. Women LOVE to be pursued. By hooking up you are taking away this natural and important process to finding love and commitment. We believe you can get to know someone on many different levels in a "one-on-one" relationship that you won't ever experience in a group setting. Also, in these groups, you will never develop the element of romance that you can when it's just the two of you. Courting has worked in affairs of the heart for centuries, why are some of you so willing to cheapen this tradition by treating each other with a complete lack of respect, consideration and commitment? Both parties deserve more than just a casual hook up. Each of you deserves to be special to each other and you can only do this by being called out of the group. Don't reinvent the wheel, Jack and Jane. Dating still does work and can be even more fun!

Ain't Nothing Like the Real Thing

If you look at dating as writing your own lyrics that speaks your language of love and think like a musician, you'd be surprised how suddenly you become a star. We really want you to see that to be successful you have to put some time and effort in your writing. It's important to prepare and condition yourself before you can cut a new CD (or for some of us, we still remember them being called an album). But before you get started you need to understand what it takes to become a successful song writer. Developing your own style and personality is very easy. We will teach you just how to do that and keep you singing forever.

What's Going On?

Let's look at defining what dating actually means:

Dat'ing [standard definition] "Dating is any social activity performed as a pair or even a group with the aim of each assessing the other's suitability as their partner in an intimate relationship or as a spouse. The word refers to the act of agreeing on a time and 'date' when a pair can meet and engage in some social activity."

While we would agree that the above definition describes fairly accurately what dating is supposed to be, we think it doesn't quite ring true with most people's experiences. We are assuming you have sought out our advice because the following definition more accurately describes your dating experiences:

Dat'ing [our definition] **1** to be dancing in the streets only to find you're on opposite one ways; **2** to be subjected to a blind date and wish you had a blind fold; **3** to feel like a clown or be dating one; **4** to march to the beat of a drum while they march to the beat of . . . something else.

If this does, in fact, more accurately describe your dating experiences, we completely understand and empathize with your plight. Having experienced some of our own dating missteps, we are here to tell you that there is hope. We want to share with you our wisdom and knowledge gained from our own personal dating experiences, as well as the many others who have shared with us their stories of success and failure. Just know that you are certainly not alone and help is on the way!

Stop! In the Name of Love

Having a negative attitude can severely cripple your dating life. We've all experienced bad dates or have listened to the horror stories from our friends. It's amazingly easy to develop a negative attitude about the entire process, especially if you have been hit hard and had the wind knocked out of you. However, you must drop the "baggage" from the past to move successfully into the future. Baggage can be described as bitterness, anger, resentment and feeling scorned. These can be difficult to purge from your mind, body and soul. If you don't release yourself from these negative feelings, you will find it difficult to go forward in dating. One of the most important changes you can make in preparing yourself for successful dating is to reverse that negative or poor attitude to a positive one.

Some signs that point to a negative attitude may include talking trash of the opposite sex or saying things like "why bother, it never works out anyway." Sitting home alone on a Saturday night is okay once in a while, but if you find yourself avoiding social opportunities excessively, this can also be a sign that you need an attitude adjustment. Any one of these examples will leave you singing the blues instead of a love song.

> "Did you know that the single most important thing you can do to make yourself more approachable is SMILE?"

Don't Leave Me This Way

It is in your best interest to put the past behind you before starting any new dating experiences. Here are some strategies that may help you move past any prior painful breakups:

1. Find time to spend with family and friends. They can provide emotional support during a tough break up. Talking through your feelings is necessary in the healing process.

2. Get back into your own game, which can help you sort through your feelings during an emotional time. Examples may include: (1) going away for a long weekend by yourself or with your buddies; (2) start up a home project (e.g., finish your basement, redecorate your bedroom); or (3) dive into a beloved hobby.

3. Do things that make you feel good about yourself. Build your self confidence by going back to the gym and getting those endorphins moving. Also, get rid of some of your old clothing and buy yourself a few new outfits so you can start with a fresh new look.

4. De-cluttering and cleaning your house can be great therapy. Purging your house of the clutter can help you also purge the clutter from your mind. This will help you de-stress and then be able to focus on your new direction in life and dating.

These strategies can help you process prior losses and help develop your game plan for a brand new beginning. Note, however, if these negative feelings are deep rooted, it may be necessary for you to seek some professional help in order to get past them.

I'm Coming Out

Now, not everyone has a bad attitude. Some of you just simply don't know how to write a love song. So, the first thing you need to do is put together your strategy. What is your plan to meet the opposite sex? Your initial strategy would be to assess your own personality and what approach to meeting people best suits you.

If you are on the shy side, you might feel more comfortable with on-line dating, which gives you a sense of ease in being able to talk through email prior to meeting. Another easy approach might be joining a group that does activities you enjoy like travel groups, biking groups, or a pottery class.

If you are more outgoing and social, you might find a karaoke or sports bar is fun. You may want to involve yourself in organizations that plan social events for a charity or a cause of your choice. On-line dating can also be good for you because you're not afraid to meet a variety of new and interesting people.

Reach Out I'll Be There

A possible prospect could be anybody you come in contact with any time of the day so you must be prepared. Every time you come into contact with someone, you should approach it as an opportunity to possibly meet someone you might like to date. We have heard stories about people meeting at grocery stores, gas stations and the corner store. When you are standing in line or at the pump, why not strike up a conversation with that Jack or Jane who's doing the same thing? Generally, we know very quickly whether we find someone attractive to us, so why not take the chance? While these are very brief encounters, they can be great opportunities to give them a business card (make sure your email address is on it). You can then chat a few times to see if there is any substance to that brief encounter. Note: if you don't have any business cards, get some! Remember, though, for them to work, you have to carry them at all times. Keep some in the car, your purse or wallet! This way you're always prepared to meet the girl or guy of your dreams.

Remember, though, SAFETY FIRST! If you meet someone in a situation described above, use some common sense here. Make sure if you choose to meet them again it's in a public place, you let at least one person know where you are going to be, and carry your cell phone. Treat it just like you would if you met someone on-line.

AIN'T NO MOUNTAIN HIGH ENOUGH

> "Did you know that if you lean in close and hold their gaze during the conversation, it shows you're interested?"

Other places you may find a potential date: Favorite biking trails, the book store, a dog park, concerts, sporting events, art museums, parties, and for some of you, even the mall! The list is endless so be prepared to meet someone any place at any time.

It Takes Two

Talk to the opposite sex as much as possible. The more you talk to the opposite sex, the more you will learn and feel more confident in being around them. This will go a long way in sharpening your skills for successful dating. We suggest you set a goal of talking to three new people of the opposite sex every week. These certainly do not need to all be potential dates, but they will help you get into the head of a potential date. Feel free to ask your friends how they met their significant others. This will help you get some ideas on where and how to meet people.

Communication skills are very important and talking to as many people as possible will help in honing those skills. The most attractive quality for the opposite sex is confidence. The more you talk to people, the more relaxed you will become around them and this will build confidence. It's important to just be yourself! Remember, this is a process, so allow yourself the time to sharpen those skills. There are no shortcuts so practice, practice, and more practice!

Now that you have gotten your head into shape, what about the rest of you? If you have packed on a couple of extra lbs, we suggest you hit the gym! You can never go wrong with putting some sweat into your daily routine. You may need to do some sit ups, push ups, pull ups, and whatever other "ups" necessary to pick yourself up and get back into shape! Exercise is great in helping your positive physical and mental outlook so even if you're thin, you need it too! There is nothing like getting those endorphins coursing through your system to make you feel great! When you feel great, the positive energy will flow out of you and will attract your favorite Jack or Jane to you.

CHAPTER 2

Smiling Faces . . . Sometimes

We hope that you have practiced your communication skills and are now prepared to start moving to your own music. In this chapter we will provide you with instructions on (1) how to assess whether your prospect is receptive to your advances . . . or not (2) how to approach someone new with confidence, and (3) how to execute a winning opening line. Please note that we have broken this chapter into two parts. The first is for you Jack and the second is for you Jane. We think it's important to know the other songs in the jukebox so make sure you read this entire chapter.

> **"Did you know that you will kill any chances for a date if your opening line is "what's your sign"?"**

For You, Jack

I Can't Get Next to You

One of the more frequently asked questions is: "How do I meet someone?" While every guy is different, most can still benefit from using the same techniques. In most cases, you guys should take the lead in initiating the first contact. Given that, your approach to meeting someone will differ from a woman's approach, which is why we have opted to isolate your information. The following techniques, while not all encompassing, should give you enough information to at least get you started and heading in the right direction.

Reading the Interest Cues

Could it be that she doesn't like me (for real)?

Scenario A - You've joined some friends at the local sports bar, you're feeling good, looking good, and in walks a woman you find attractive. She sits at a table with some girlfriends. She glances your way, but there is no eye contact for any length of time. She is simply scanning the room. She goes back to talking with her friends and never looks your way again. Now, we understand that you may feel attracted to her, but, a glance is a glance as a dance is a dance.

Is she interested? Our advice: If you try to catch her attention and it's just not happening, we would suggest you move on as your advance will most likely be turned down.

Scenario B - You're at a friend's party at their home and she walks in and you think, "Wow!" You ask your friend who she is and would they introduce you. After being introduced, you chat for a few moments; however, she's looking around the room, keeping her replies brief and doesn't further the conversation. She may even try to bring others into the conversation, focusing more attention on them. Or, after a few moments, she excuses herself.

Is she interested? Our advice: If there's no flow in conversation, flow on to someone else.

Could it be that she likes me?

Back to Scenario A -You've joined some friends at the local sports bar, you're feeling good, looking good, and in walks a woman you find attractive. She sits at a table with some girlfriends. She glances your way and stops briefly to smile at you. She goes back to talking with her friends, but continues to look in your direction to see if you may be glancing her way. If you are and you linger long enough to smile and she returns the smile again, the game is on!

Is she interested? Our advice: Move on to the approach/opening line.

Back to Scenario B - You're at a friend's party at their home. She walks in and you think, "Wow!" You ask your friend who she is and would they introduce you. After being introduced, you chat for a few moments, during which, she will ask questions about you and will show interest. She smiles and laughs a lot and doesn't seem to be in a hurry to move away. If others join the conversation, she's polite, but always brings it back to you. You have her attention . . . attention . . . attention.

Is she interested? Our advice: This is a great opportunity! Don't let the next Jack grab it away from you!

> "Did you know that Jane believes that men who wear the color blue are more stable and faithful?"

How to Initiate an Appropriate Approach

You have established that there is some interest, now, what do you do?

In the sports bar scenario: Okay, Jack, this is a lost art. Whatever happened to buying a lady a drink? I mean, really, how hard can this be? You ask the wait-ress to walk over and ask her what she's drinking and you pay for it! This is a great way to break the ice and won't break the bank! Step up to the plate for good-ness sake and Man Up! She will appreciate the effort and it will give her a reason to either walk up to you or give you a signal to approach her so she can say thank you.

At the party scenario: If you notice her drink is low, ask what she's drinking and if you may re-fill it. Note! Remember what she is drinking. During the conver-sation, pay attention to her outside interests. You now have an opportunity to suggest that you do something she likes, together (e.g., the theater, skiing, art fairs, mountain biking, well, you get the picture). Another note, don't feign interest in what she likes to do, find a mutual interest!

That Pesky Opening Line

You have initiated your approach and the first thing out of your mouth is crucial! So, let's take note of the Do's and Don'ts.

DON'T say things like "If I told you I loved your body, would you hold it against me?" Or, "Did you wash your jeans in Windex because I can see myself in them?" Please don't insult her intelligence! Trust us; you won't have a shot with a line like that! Not only are they unimaginative opening lines, it makes you appear to be a womanizer (and not a very good one). It also makes you come off as juvenile and lacking intelligence.

DO say things like "You have such a presence about you." Or, "You lit up the room when you walked in." These types of opening lines show intelligence, respect, and are genuine compliments. Above all, remember that by showing respect for her by what you say and how you act, you will come across as a gentleman. Women always enjoy meeting a gentleman!

For You, Jane

I Second that Emotion

Back in the 1960's, girls used to sit by the phone, listening to Diana Ross and the Supremes, waiting for their favorite Jack to call. Women today still generally wait for the man to initiate contact. It's not to say that we haven't come a long way in equality for women (gratefully), however, most women still like to have a man chase them. In light of this, a woman's approach to meeting men is different from a man's. As indicated above, we have chosen to focus on each approach separately. The first thing you need to do is to learn how to read a man's body language.

Reading the Interest Cues

Could it be that he doesn't like me? Dang!

Scenario A - You're at a local pub with some friends and in walks a guy who strikes your fancy. So now what? If indeed you are keeping an open mind about possibly meeting someone, then we recommend that you sit at the bar or gather near a stand up table. This puts you in a more social location and you will be more approachable (beware, ladies, generally, men won't approach a group of girls huddled together at a table). So, a guy sits down at the bar a ways from you. He glances briefly at you, but continues to scan the room and doesn't really look your way again.

Is he interested? Our advice: We think he should be considered simply eye candy. Enjoy the view and move on.

Scenario B – You're at a friend's party and in walks a guy you find attractive and you think, "Wow!" So you ask the host/hostess to make an introduction. You initiate a conversation and he virtually doesn't reply or he keeps his replies to a minimum. This is not a good sign. Men can often be brutal and direct in these situations and may simply walk away. If this happens, don't take it personally, he's just not interested. You don't want to go after someone who is so plainly not "in" to you. A note here, this does not mean that you are in any way unattractive! It can be as simple as you not being his type or he is taken.

Is he interested? Our advice: Men are natural born hunters and they will pursue you in an obvious way right from the start. This guy is looking for other game, don't waste your time.

Could it be that he likes me? Yippee!

Back to Scenario A – You're at a local pub with some friends and in walks a guy who strikes your fancy. So now what? We are assuming you are sitting at the bar or some other approachable location and he sits within close proximity. He glances at you and smiles or makes some other positive gesture toward you (e.g., he may wink at you or nod his head in acknowledgment). You smile back and notice that he continues to look your way and tries to capture your attention.

Is he interested? Our advice: This guy is interested! Move on to "How to get them to approach you."

Back to Scenario B - You're at a friend's party and in walks a guy you find attractive and you think, "Wow!" So you ask the host/hostess to make an introduction. If he is interested, he may check you out from head to toe. Men are visual creatures so we consider this to be a good sign if it's done in a complimentary way. So don't be put off by it provided that he continues a conversation with you in a positive, respectful manner. Most men will make sure that they keep your attention with direct eye contact and (we hope) stimulating conversation.

Is he interested? Our advice: Yes, it's definitely moving in a positive direction and if you are interested too, this is not the time to play hard to get. Make sure you let him know that you find him interesting.

How to Get Them to Approach You

You have established that there is interest so how do you get them to approach you?

We know that you, Jane, will not believe us when we tell you that you have way more power than you give yourself credit for. In the bar scenario, for example, we feel that good old fashioned flirting is a lost art. Men do not like being rejected any more than women. You have to give them that comfort zone that you will be receptive to their advance. How about winking at him or, perhaps a cute smile and finger wave? This will get a positive reaction and will usually motivate him to either approach you or at least buy you a drink.

"Jane, did you know that you should apply fragrance to the bend in the elbow, back of the knee, the wrist, the neck and your cleavage?"

How to Flirt

Let's get back to the lost art of flirting, as we want you to come off as classy and lady-like so we have a couple of tips for you. While engaging in a mutually interesting conversation, make sure you maintain eye contact and smile. Laughter is the staple of flirting, so laugh it up and have fun. You can also try swiping your fingers through your hair or try batting your eyes at him. Here's a good one, put on some lip gloss in a slightly provocative manner (don't overdo this one as you may come off as silly or even trashy). You want flirting to be sexy and sophisticated. Men also find confidence to be extremely sexy so if you find these forms of flirting we have suggested not exactly your style, then feel free to find your own sense of creativity. Come on Jane, flirt it up!

CHAPTER 3

What Does it Take (to Win Your Love)?

Statistics show that more than 50% of singles are currently using an on-line dating source to get dates. One of the most crucial aspects of getting dates through this method is ensuring that your profile attracts the kind of person you are interested in. We will be providing you with some helpful tips and instructions so that you don't scratch your album or drop your CD before you even hear the music.

Reasons for Turning to On-Line Dating

1. You work a lot of hours.

2. You're not having luck meeting anyone (the grocery store and church just aren't working like my Aunt Bess said it would).

3. You're not meeting the kind of quality people you're looking for.

4. It is hard for you to strike up a conversation with a complete stranger.

5. You are lacking in self-confidence or are too shy and you find that emailing first is a more comfortable approach.

6. It is a way for you to weed out the toads from the princes/divas from the girls next door.

7. You like to be in control of whom you want to date and how fast you want it to move along.

8. You like to date a lot of people.

Warning! Be Prepared for Some Tough Straight Talk in this Section!

How to Create an On-Line Dating Profile

There are a lot of choices today in on-line dating websites. The first thing that you need to find out is which site is likely to have members that are the type of people you are looking for. Beware! There are a lot of goofy and freaky websites out there. So, unless you are looking for goofy and freaky, be careful where you tread. You could find yourself confronted with an array of colorful people with unusual fetishes. Know what type of site you are signing on to!

First, and most importantly, don't even try to set up a profile without a recent, updated photo of what you <u>really</u> look like. It's only fair to let others honestly see what you look like as most will let you see their true selves.

Things to Remember When Selecting Your Photo(s)

<u>No sunglasses or hats – why?</u>

Because you're hiding behind your sunglasses and your hat so they can't really see what you look like. Let people see you because as the old song goes, "everybody's beautiful in their own way!" If you are sincere about meeting someone, be honest about what you look like. They will see you anyway at some point. Just be upfront! We recommend that you include both a full body shot as well as a close up that's clear. In most cases, if you try to deceive someone about the way you look, when they do finally meet you, not only will they feel misled and possibly angry, you'll be humiliated and won't get a second date. So, what have you gained? Not a thing!

No dead animals should ever be in the photo with you!

We understand that a lot of you guys have an overload of testosterone, but really Jack, Jane could care less that you're a hunter. It's not something that most women find attractive. In fact, most women feel a level of discomfort in looking at blood and guts. It can come off as uncompassionate and lacking in any sort of sensitivity. Now, there is a chance you could capture the attention of a female hunter, but those odds are very low. Now, if you're looking for a guy to go hunting with, then we would say your ball is going straight down the alley heading for a strike! If not, we suggest you leave those photos out of your dating profile.

Hey, which one are you?

This is not fun when trying to figure out which one you are in the large group photo and, unless we have bionic eyeballs, we generally can't really see you even if we do figure out which one you are. Oh, yeah, you're the one in the blue shirt next the one wearing the other blue shirt way in the back. Need we say more? Make sure you are alone or at most, with one other person (clarifying which one you are). Again, make it a close up and be sure it's recent (within the last year).

Clothing, clothing, clothing.

We think you should have some on! Let's address Jane first. If you struggle in the fashion arena (there is no shame in this), we advise you to ask a friend who will be honest with you. You don't want to come across as cheesy, sleazy, or trashy. If you're going to expose yourself, the type of man you're going to attract will be looking for a good time, not a good relationship. Beware of the man who asks that you submit a bikini shot, he's more interested in sex than he is in you. So, don't be so naïve!

Okay, now for you Jack. It's not that we don't love a great chest on a guy, but flaunting it makes you look like your ego is as big as your biceps. Women can tell that you have a nice physique even if you're fully clothed. And, for you guys who don't have a great physique and want to show it off . . . please don't! You'll get a lot further ahead with a nice shirt on that's buttoned to just under your neck. The days of disco are over so we really don't want to see the shirt unbuttoned down to your navel. Please keep that shag carpet under wraps for now! Sorry, Jack, but it's true!

Hairstyles, make up, etc.

Less is more! Don't get too carried away with the "pump your hair up" products. You don't want to end up looking like Bozo's big top as you will surely attract a clown! Keep the hair calm, refined, yet stylish. If you haven't been to the salon/barber recently, it's time to go! Now for those of you who don't have any . . . hair, that is and you feel slightly insecure about it, play on your other assets like your beautiful smile, your nice eyes, or your excellent personal style. However, guys, we think bald is beautiful and we love you too!

Getting back to Bozo, too much makeup will certainly entertain the crowd, but not exactly in the way that you'd like. Again, less is more. Let the essence of you shine through and the rest will fall into place.

> **"Did you know that many men <u>don't</u> find it sexy if your clothes are too tight?"**

Let's Talk About Your Screen Name/Profile Handle

This should be about 4–7 words that accompany your photograph and your personal profile. Here is where you need to stand out and consider this to be a "first impression" if you will. You know that they say you never get a second chance to make a first impression, so be snappy, pizzazzy, and show off your amazing style. Avoid those that come off sounding as though you barely got through high school, such as "Are you the one?"; "Where have you been all of my life?"; "Wanna get married?"; "Looking for my other half"; or "Looking for a Mr. or Miss Hottie." UGGG! These are devoid of any intellect or substance whatsoever! This exercise should warrant some thought so take the time to really think it through. Here are a couple of suggestions that we think make the right impression: "Looking to share memories that we make together." This says that you are interested in finding a relationship with substance and longevity. We also like "Intelligence, laughter, and adventure - that's for me!" This says to us that you are looking for an adventurous relationship that's full of intellect, yet is playful and fun. One last one, "I'm baaaac-cckkk and better than before!" This shows you have a lot of self-confidence and you are not allowing the past trip ups in life to dictate your future. Of course, we expect you to use your own imagination and creativity to express who you are.

Likes and Dislikes

You're always going to lessen your chances of finding a quality person if you are too picky. For example, indicating you only will date those men or women with brown hair and blue eyes, will decrease the number of potential prospects significantly. Try to be as open and broad minded as possible, within your personal tolerance level. If you are very active and insist that they are not over-weight or are a non-smoker, that's fine because these factors can be an issue down the road. However, remember, that you're not perfect either so if you're a few pounds overweight, then you should be careful not to insist that your potential date be a hard body – this applies to both Jack and Jane. Here's a suggestion, before you sit down to fill out your likes and dislikes, perhaps you ought to strip down in front of your own mirror and take a good, hard, honest look at yourself before you make demands on how someone else should look!

Faith, Religion, and Spirituality

This can potentially be a deal breaker. If you are a person of strong faith, be honest and don't compromise this because eventually it may cause conflicts. For example, if you go to church regularly and you are looking for someone who will attend with you, but then down the road you find out that they are not into the church going thing, you will end up being very disappointed. Here's a tip, depending on your faith, there are many dating web sites that are geared toward particular faith based groups. You may find that to be the best place to start. At the very least, be clear in your description that you are of a particular faith and looking for someone whose beliefs are the same.

The Truth Must be Told

<u>Children</u>

If you have children, you absolutely should never lie or lead people to believe that you don't. Leaving this area blank is the same thing as lying. They will figure it out eventually and you will be dubbed as untrustworthy, not to mention, a terrible person. The fact that you could denounce your own children for the sake of finding someone to date is simply intolerable and any person with half a brain should run for the hills. If you have grown children who are living on their own, you should still indicate that you have children. Most sites will give you an option to indicate that they are older and not living with you. Besides if you meet someone who doesn't want kids, what are you going to do, put your kids in the closet every time they come over? Geez, come on, just be honest here.

Smoking

Now, we don't get this "occasionally" option on whether you smoke that we've seen on some of the dating web sites. If you select this option, here's the truth, you SMOKE! Don't try to hide the fact that you smoke. Trust us! We were all born with noses. Noses, biologically, have the purpose of smelling. You will smell like smoke, so we will figure it out! And, you may not realize it, but those of us that don't smoke can smell it a mile away. Also, for those non-smokers, kissing a smoker is like kissing an ashtray! Ick! If you smoke, say you smoke. If you don't and don't want to date a smoker, be emphatic that you are looking for a non-smoker. Let the person who's looking at your profile know the truth, so they can decide.

Drinking

When you select the "socially" option, what we believe this to mean is when you are out, you may have a drink or two. Socially, does not mean getting drunk every time you go out on a date. There is also an option for "often." What we believe this to mean is that you pretty much drink three to four times per week or even daily. If that's you, be honest as you may find someone who likes their evening cocktails as well.

Weight:

Now come on! How do you think you're going to pull this off when you finally meet and you are 25 lbs over the "slim" option you selected? There are plenty of men and women who don't put the emphasis on weight. You will end up looking like a big fat liar (pun intended) and people can be cruel. You may put yourself in a situation where you are humiliated. Not worth it! We are not trying to be mean, but are trying to warn you of what could come your way if you're not being totally honest.

Age

Now this really gets our goat! A person lies about their age and you agree to meet them. So, you're sitting at coffee and you're thinking, "hmmm, he or she doesn't really look 42, they look a bit older." So, they say, "You know, I have to be honest about something. I'm not normally a liar, but I lied on my profile about my age, I'm really 52." Okay, this is our quandary. I'm not really a liar? But yet, I lied? In this particular incident, this person gave the explanation that they still wanted to have children and felt that by identifying their real age, they were attracting prospects that were already beyond childbearing years or past the point of wanting to have children. Of course, most websites allow you to write a paragraph or two about who you are and what you are looking for. Wouldn't it have been prudent to simply state that they were looking for someone who wants to have children as most people read these paragraphs? Those who were not interested in having children would have moved on. There is no excuse for lying no matter what your reasoning is!

> **"Don't forget to compliment her or him!"**

Your Self Description

Here is where you have an opportunity to express in writing who you are. It's okay to be confident and have great self-esteem, but be careful that you are not bragging or boasting. Please remember, ladies and gentlemen, this is not an interview for the corner office job. While we think it's great you have so many accomplishments, we are more interested in who you are on the inside. It is far more interesting and attractive to read about someone who gives back to the community or is involved in some kind of charity work. Please feel free to express this to its fullest potential. Most people admire and appreciate people who are compassionate, empathetic, and have a giving heart.

Be creative in this area of your profile. Try to set yourself apart from the others (not too far off, though, that you completely go off the map). Also, people like fun people so make this a bit humorous if you can, as people love to laugh. A tip, once you have completed the description, we recommend that you have someone you trust read it for you and ask for their feedback. If you have someone that is of the opposite sex willing to read it and help you out, this would be even better. This will help greatly if you are unsure of how you are coming across. Your trusted friend may point out something fantastic about you that you may have overlooked or they will point out some common errors that you may have missed.

What You're Looking For

Now, let's be real! No one is perfect, so asking for "perfect" is just plain ridiculous. For example, Jack may write, "I am looking for tall, thin, gorgeous, highly educated, successful, and can contribute financially to the relationship." Wow, what a perfect world this would be if you could actually find a Jane who meets all of those demands. Wait, why would they need you? So, if you're looking for this woman, we assume that you are tall, dark, handsome, and independently wealthy. Aren't you? Probably not! So seriously take a look at yourself before you determine the kind of woman you're looking for. There's no point in doing on-line dating if you set your expectations so high that no real woman can possibly meet them. Maybe 1% of the population may meet these qualifications and they are already taken! Ha!

Another big NO, NO! Please do not talk about sex in any way, shape or form in your profile. If that's all you're looking for, go to a site that is more designed around just that. Have some self-control and respect for the women reading your profile. A common mistake is that men will write things like "I love to kiss or I like to cuddle." Please, give us a break! That just sounds corny! It's a complete turnoff to any reasonably intelligent woman, so save the sex talk for a more appropriate time.

Now, Jane, it's pretty much the same for you. As we all played with Barbie dolls and we had the perfect house, clothes, car and our husband was Mr. Perfect, Ken, we know that this would be the ideal fantasy. But, really, the key word here is "fantasy." Unless you are the type of gal that meets the qualifications we described in the paragraph above, we suggest that you too be realistic in your expectations. Now a sure fire way to make a man run is to mention anything about marriage and wanting someone to take care of you in every way, as in total security. This says to a man, marry me, pay all my bills, and be the daddy to my babies and I don't really care about you as a person. This also comes off sounding like you are on a time crunch to get your life's checklist completed (a.k.a. the biological time clock). Oh, and you ladies that are single moms, be careful that you don't come across like you are desperate to find a man to take care of you and your children. Trust us, Jack will pick up on this very quickly and you could end up losing the interest of someone who might be a good match. Here again, just have some fun and keep it light!

We know we've beaten you up a little here, so we'll give you a few tips that we think work.

Really give some thought about what kind of man or woman (beyond the physical attributes) that you are looking for and focus on those qualities. We suggest that you just pick the top two or three qualities that are most important to you (not ten, which will end up significantly reducing your chances of having anyone respond to you). You can also express specifics like, someone who likes to cook, or likes cycling, or likes to travel, etc. One of our favorites is when you say "I'm looking for someone who shares my interests and wants to create memories together." That says to us that you are interested in someone beyond a few dates as well as looking past minor flaws, because we all have them.

Everyone likes a sense of humor so it doesn't have to be so serious; however, be sure not to force the humor, just let it come out naturally. No one likes to be dictated to, so make sure you are not coming off like it is a list of demands. Another good one is "I'm looking for someone who has a sense of humor and works in finding laughter in the day to day bumps in the road." This says that you take things lightly and aren't going to run at the first sign of trouble. Remember, balance is very important in this section, meaning that this description should be more of an "essay" so make sure you include some things about what you are willing to give to the relationship. You don't want to come off as self-centered and only interested in what they can give to you. For example, stating that "You'd love to work together to help fulfill their hearts desires" says that you are willing to be an active partner in the relationship.

Put some thought into this but make sure it isn't your entire life story. It should be longer than one sentence, but not 12 paragraphs. We recommend you keep it to one good-sized paragraph that hits the highlights. Put in a little effort in being creative, imaginative, and have fun!

One last note, Use SPELLCHECK! Nothing is worse than reading a profile laden with misspelled words! It makes you appear uneducated, when it really could be that you simply don't type well. Don't make this common mistake!

Dating Communications (Emails up to First Meeting)

Your communications should be more than just one or two lines. Put a little effort into these emails, however, they don't have to be novels either. Use a little common sense. A paragraph or two is more than sufficient. Tell them something about yourself, but don't forget to ask them a question that will invoke a response so as to keep the conversation flowing. Make these emails interesting. One of our favorite questions to ask is "where do you see yourself in ten years?" This type of question can generate a lot of conversation and you can get a feel for their mindset and where they are heading in their life. If you are looking for more than just a date, it's important to state that you are looking for a relationship that can be built upon over time. This is a good way to establish that you're not interested in a "game player" or someone who is thinking much more short-term, if indeed you are not. Why waste anyone's time? Also, open your heart when you write. For some this is easy, for others it's more difficult. However, by letting someone see into your heart, you will have a much greater chance of drawing the right person to you. Now, a tip, don't get too carried away and say you want to get married soon, which will more likely scare someone away who isn't yet ready for that step. Again, keep it light and fun.

These communications should be fairly short-lived, prior to the first meeting. Sometimes people want to email for way too long before meeting. It's too hard to establish whether there is chemistry without a face-to-face meeting. Most of us don't want to spend months and months just emailing. It seems like a big waste of your time when you could be moving on to someone who is more open to meeting you and wanting to possibly begin a relationship. We would caution you that someone who is too hesitant to meet may be hiding something. Rather than continuing to be frustrated with their lack of initiative, we suggest you move on.

> "Sex on the first date is great . . .
> if you never want to see them again!"

Where to Meet

<u>Always better to be safe than sorry</u>! We can't say that enough. Please choose a public place to meet and somewhere in familiar territory (as in close to your home, especially, for you Jane). Always make sure that someone you trust knows who and where you are meeting. If you have additional information about the person you're meeting (e.g., phone number(s), work place, an address, etc.), give that information to them as well. You can never be too safe! Always have your cell phone fully charged and on your person at all times. It's best to

WHAT DOES IT TAKE (TO WIN YOUR LOVE)?

leave it on, but you can set it on "silence/vibrate" mode so as to not be interrupted during the date. We would recommend a coffee house (rather than a bar or restaurant) so that it can be brief in case you determine that you are not interested. Also, mixing alcohol and first meetings can cloud your thinking and lead you astray. Don't be foolish!

For your own sake (and theirs), we recommend that you plan to keep the first meeting very short. When we say, short, we mean 15 minutes over a quick cup of coffee. How do you do that, you ask? Tell your date that you have a short time to meet up for coffee because you have other plans but would like to at least have a quick greeting for now. Most people know within 5 minutes whether there is any chemistry. So, if you're meeting doesn't go as well as you had hoped and the chemistry just isn't there, you have your out. Why stay any longer than necessary? It's a waste of time for both you and your prospective date. Now, if you find that there is something there, then you can extend it by simply saying that you have a little more time than you originally thought. We, however, highly recommend you keep it to an hour at most as this will leave them wanting more.

CHAPTER 4

Super Freak

W e want you to be successful in creating your own Motown sound so be sure not to fall into these ten avoidable traps. Don't get caught lip sinking when you can develop your own true voice. Below are the ten deadly sins, which we highly recommend you avoid. Don't put these nails in your coffin!

1. Being Late

What does this say about you right from the beginning? So, out of the gate, you run right into the wall! Wow, that was a grand entrance! One that will not only get you remembered, but will also get you a grand exit.

This will say a lot about you as a first impression and as we all know you don't get a second chance for one of those. You will come across as being ill prepared and narcissistic. Your date's time is just as important as yours so if you are truly interested, be on time! It's really not that hard if you try.

2. Lying

What did your mother say about lying? It will only trap you in the web you spin. The truth always comes to the surface at some point so just be honest to begin with. That way, you won't look like a fool later. We guarantee that if you get caught telling an obvious lie, you will have no hope of getting to a second date and rightly so. We find that some people lie about things that they cannot possibly keep hidden for any length of time. For example, your age, your weight, children, marriages, etc. Really, do you think that once someone discovers you've lied that they will want to continue any kind of relationship with you? Look, it's not cool! We don't like it, so just don't do it!

3. Poor Personal Hygiene and Bad Breath

We know that some of you are saying, you're kidding right? Unfortunately, we are not. There are some men and women who just haven't been acquainted with a bar of soap for some time. Okay, for you Jack, do the three "S's" (if you don't know what they are, here it is: shxx, shower and shave). Now, for you Jane, do the three "P's" (i.e., primp, powder and perfume). For bad breath, we recommend you floss and brush and, hey, live a little dangerously and go ahead and gargle too! Before you get out of the car and approach your date's door, do the breath check and make sure you're carrying your handy, dandy breath mints.

4. Very Poor Manners

Okay, sloppy Joe, we are talking to you! This makes for a great dish, but not a dish we want to date! Let's go back to Charm School 101. Burping loudly after dinner is not a compliment! It's just plain gross, so unless you are 10 years old, save it for a time with the boys! For you female race horse fans, try not chewing your gum like you're heading for the finish line at the Kentucky Derby, chomp, chomp, chomp! Sounds like a cow chewing cud. That's not how you want to be remembered, is it? For both you, Jack and Jane, shoveling large portions of food in your mouth or loudly slurping your beverage is truly not attractive. Try to be a bit more circumspect in your eating and drinking habits. A tip, make sure you tuck, zip, and button before leaving the bathroom. Oh, and, by the way, please wash your hands before returning to the table. Ewh! One last note, try to get through at least the first date without using any cuss words! Or, we will have to borrow that soap we wanted you to use in number 3 above, and stick it in your mouth!

5. Excessively Answering Your Cell Phone/ Text Messaging

We think technology is wonderful . . . when you're at work or at home on your own couch! On a date, it's just plain annoying and rude! If you'd rather spend more time on your phone with your friends than being on a date, wouldn't the obvious choice be to not go on a date? Your friends can live without you for a couple hours, seriously! You're not all that important! Sorry! We don't think we need to say anymore, right?

"Looking good is as important as feeling comfortable!"

6. Interrogating Your Date Rather Than Letting the Conversation Flow

Unless you want your date to feel like they are sitting in a dark room with a spot light in their face, the FBI circling and pelting them with a barrage of questions, we suggest you temper your enthusiastic inquiries. You don't need to know everything on the first date. Take a breath! Your date will feel very uncomfortable if you just keep asking one question after another, barely giving them time to supply a brief response. At least give them a chance to answer the first one before hitting them with second one. Conversation should be a two way street, with some give and take. Give them time to ask a few questions of their own. This is supposed to be fun. It shouldn't feel like you are on an interview. Just relax and take your time in getting to know someone. A little mystery is very intriguing. By leaving something to the imagination, you will leave the door open to having topics to share on future dates.

7. Going on, and on, and on About Your Ex and/or Children

Everyone loves death by chocolate! Death by date, though, is defined as you talking ad nauseam about your ex (poor you, get over it!) and your wonderful, darling (to you) children. It's okay to share that you have children, but we don't care what funny little thing Johnny said this morning at breakfast. At this point, it is about you and your date, not you and the "others." Seriously, if you need to continue to talk about your ex, in particular, find a friend or a therapist, as your date is neither at this point. Again, this is a date, not a therapy session or daycare. There is plenty of time, should you get that far, to discuss these subjects more in-depth.

8. Being a Chatterbox

Let's start with you Jane, since this is something that Jack really dislikes. If you are sounding like a typewriter going 90 words a minute, droning on, and on, and on, they will tune you OUT! They will no longer hear a word you say as you continue on your journey of verbiage. For the first five minutes, they are listening, after that, you're done. Please, take it slow and relax. We know that women have a tendency to get over-excited and want to share . . . everything. Women worry when there might be a lull in the conversation and feel compelled to fill the silence; however, give him a moment to digest what you are saying so that he can formulate a response. Remember, as we said in paragraph 6 above, leaving something to mystery will keep them coming back for more and that my dears is the whole idea, yes?

For you Jack, you don't necessarily talk fast, but we hear complaints all the time that you talk too much about yourself. This to women comes across as you being very self-absorbed and not interested in them as much as you just wanting to hear yourself talk. Over time, they will see who you are and will come to know your accomplishments. You really don't need to brag, okay? A tip, it's very attractive to be humble.

9. Getting Drunk

If you're an alcoholic, well, this might be a bit of a challenge and we recommend you seek some help. If you're not an alcoholic, don't let your nerves get the best of you and overdue it. We all know that alcohol can provide some liquid courage; however, there is a fine line between calming one's nerves and making a fool of yourself. This first impression gives your date the per-ception that you have no control or that you possibly have a drinking problem. It can start out as just having some fun but can get ugly very fast. We know mixing alcohol with certain types of personalities can be toxic. They can become loud, obnoxious and even abusive. So we caution you when dating, it might be wise to temper your drinking and pace yourself. Here's a tip, have a glass of water in between each alcoholic beverage. This should help keep you from over-drinking.

10. The Attack Kiss

No one likes to be cornered when they don't want to be. So, unless you are completely assured that your date wants to be kissed, we suggest you hold off that impulse for another date. You may even find that it takes more than even two dates to get to that point. Keep in mind, that your date may desire you even more if you hold off. We always want what we can't have, right? Don't assume that since they accepted a date that you have the right to slap your lips on theirs and deliver the big wet one! For Jane, anyway, you will not only turn them off completely, you'll be lucky if they don't kick you where it hurts. Kissing is not a right; it's a privilege and a very personal one at that. Simply put . . . don't rush it!

> "Jack and Jane really want someone who is trustworthy and will be there for them!"

CHAPTER 5

You Can't Hurry Love

The show is just a few hours away so let's do our sound check! Here's how the preparation should go:

7:00 a.m.   Alarm clock rings.

7:15 a.m.   Hit the snooze.

7:30 a.m.   Hit the snooze again.

7:45 a.m.   Oh, heck, hit it one more time.

8:00 a.m.   Roll out of bed with a new attitude!

8:30 a.m.   Have some coffee and a breakfast of champions (because that's what you are).

9:00 a.m.   Head for the gym or go for a brisk walk to release any stress or anxiety and get those endorphins in shape.

10:00 a.m.   Take a shower and put on your best "come hither" scent.

10:30 a.m.   Do something with your hair.

11:00 a.m.   Relax and read the paper. Get up on current events so you are prepared to discuss the day's news and world events.

12:00 noon   Time to eat a light, healthy and nutritious lunch so your body has fuel.

12:30 p.m.   Tidy up the house in case your date should be picking you up or coming to your house.

1:30 p.m.   Try to get any errands out of the way so you are not distracted with "I forgot this or that."

2:30 p.m.   Take a couple of hours to watch some TV or read a book, nap, anything that helps you recharge.

5:00 p.m.   If you are doing the driving, make sure you have a clean car (inside and out).

5:30 p.m.   Make sure you have a map to their house or the restaurant to avoid being late due to getting lost.

6:00 p.m.   Start to prepare for the date (e.g., put on the appropriate clothing according to your event).

6:30 p.m.   For you Jane, take a little extra care with the makeup and for you Jack, polish up those shoes!

7:00 p.m.   Arrive at your date's doorstep, or answer the doorbell with a smile, or arrive at the meeting location with confidence and a radiant smile.

CHAPTER 6

Baby, I'm For Real

Here is where the music starts, so turn it up! This chapter is designed to coach you through the first date song. If you follow these musical notes, you will come out at the top of the charts. Again, we have separated this chapter, Jack first - Jane second. If you want to hear the music on both radio stations, you have to tune in.

For You, Jack

Let it Whip

The first date is your opportunity to rock their world with your own personal style! If you have already met once before in person, then you've gotten past that tricky "first impression" and peaked her interest. If not, here's your chance! Again, what's appropriate conduct for you on the first date is not necessarily appropriate for her. In order that you know exactly what to do and what's expected, we are, again, focusing just on you Jack for the moment. Let's start with the basics and work our way toward the finish of a great first date.

What NOT to Wear – Seriously

We know you guys love your casual, comfy clothes! However (and this is a big however), please do not wear the clothes you did your lawn care in that day on any date, especially not the first date. For example, sweaty T-shirts are not a turn on! Even though we know that pheromones are produced from perspiration, you can be a bit overpowering. Your ripped Levi's with holes where your wallet used to be is great for around the house, but for all us girls' sake, please leave them there. By the way, those tennis shoes that you've had since high school basketball should never be worn on a date, no matter how casual. In fact, they need to be thrown out altogether.

What TO Wear

Be a leader in your own life and be willing to stand out a little bit! Take some initiative and look at the men around you and not necessarily just your friends. When you are out and about town, do some research for yourself by paying a little attention to the fashion of the men in that environment. What we mean is if you are at an upscale restaurant for example, look at what those guys are wearing. This only takes a quick glance around the room and can be very informative. If you find yourself at the mall (we know that's one of your favorite places, chuckle, chuckle), take a moment to stop at a few of the men's clothing stores and look at the displays, mannequins, and posters on the walls. You will get a great idea of what's in style and how to put the pieces together. Stop and ask the salesperson for some suggestions if you feel unsure of your own taste. For those of you who have great women in your life (e.g., sisters, sisters-in-law, mothers, friends, friends' wives, etc.) who seem to have some fashion sense, take advantage of that opportunity and ask for their help. Most women would love to help you!

The most important thing to dressing appropriately is to know where you're going. For the casual to semi-casual date, you generally can't go wrong with an updated, well fitted, pair of jeans, dress shirt or black turtleneck, leather jacket (for the cooler weather) and a nice, clean, pair of black shoes. A staple in your closet should be a classic black suit coat. You can pair this with dress shirts, turtlenecks and various types of slacks. For the more upscale place, we suggest a nice pair of slacks (i.e., no jeans, period), a contemporary dress shirt or turtleneck, paired with a suit coat and always a nice, clean pair of dress shoes.

Where to Go / What to Do

DON'T BE LATE FOR ANY REASON! Unless you're dead or bleeding!

Have a plan. Don't show up on her doorstep with no idea of where you are going and what you are doing. You should be able to tell her in advance so she has an opportunity to prepare and choose appropriate attire. The last thing a girl wants to have happen is to find herself inappropriately dressed for the occasion. So be sure to show her courtesy by letting her know what (or where) the date is ahead of time.

Don't be afraid to be creative on a first date. We are assuming at this point that you have had some conversation with this woman and have a basic idea of your mutual interests. Now, you can do something together you both like or you can try something completely new and exciting together.

A classic date goes something like this. You set a time, pick her up (or meet, if she's more comfortable with that initially), go to dinner and maybe a show. Now, this is okay and it's nice, but, if you want to make an impact or a statement, why not try something a little less "the norm."

If you really want to get to know a person, take them out of their comfort zone (within reason, guys, know your ladies). If you are athletic, for example, go for a bike ride or skiing. You could go to a shooting range (that'll get the heart pounding) or a nice walk in the park, and, hey, why not throw in a picnic basket.

Now for those of you who are stimulated intellectually, meet at a book store over coffee or go to a foreign or travel film. You may find it fun to go to a museum or science center, especially, if there is a special exhibit you both might be interested in. There is always the theater or the symphony, for those of you who enjoy the arts.

> **"Don't tell her you'll call her if you don't mean it!"**

Bring a Token of Your Affection

Here, again, is another lost art. This also does not have to cost a lot of money. A single rose is perfectly acceptable or a small box of chocolates. If you'd like to leave her with a reminder of your evening, and of you, some pretty scented hand lotion or a neat key chain are a couple great ideas. These will go a long way in setting you apart from the rest. Just a quick note here, you don't want to go overboard with this and buy some expensive gift (even if you can afford it). This should just be a "token" of your affection, nothing more. Save the bigger gifts for down the road.

The 1, 2, 3's of being a Gentleman on a Date

(1) Always open doors, including car doors. (2) Always help her with her coat. (3) Always pull her chair out for her. Don't walk 5 steps ahead of her, unless you're a prince or a king. Always ask if she has had enough to eat and drink, which would include popcorn and a beverage at the cinema's snack bar.

Yes, You Should Pay!

We know that today is a world where women are working and have money; therefore, they are willing and able to pay their own way. So, in light of this, we don't feel that you should pay all the time. She can contribute on occasion if you continue dating. But on the first date, be a gentleman and treat her like a lady, which means that you pick up the tab for the entire date, Jack!

If you don't have a lot of expendable cash, there are plenty of things that you can do that are inexpensive. Look back at the "Where to Go" section. Taking a walk and planning a little picnic basket with some cheese and crackers, doesn't cost a lot of money and can be a very nice date. In this situation, you just may have to be a little more creative, but it's doable. Not all women expect you to spend wads of cash on a date. A good portion of women are really looking for a genuine guy who is willing to make an effort in planning the date.

The Art of Conversation

This is so important! You don't want the first date to be like going on a job interview. Asking questions is certainly part of the "getting to know each other" process; however, there is room here for some creativity. Remember, you don't have to blast someone with a series of questions that prompt only a "yes" or "no" answer. You can find out about someone's interests by introducing "topics" of conversations. We realize that you have heard over and over to make it about her and not focus on yourself. This cannot be emphasized enough. Now it's not to say that you can't share in the conversation, but don't dominate it. When a topic has been introduced that seems to have sparked some interest, go deeper and, yes, we are going to say it, ask how she "feels" about it. You will get more insight into who she is when you ask how she "feels" about a subject than you ever will with a bunch of meaningless questions like "what is her favorite color?" When you're fishing for a date, listening is the hook!

All women love to be appreciated and appropriately complimented. If you are in the middle of a conversation that seems to be going well, don't stop it dead by saying "Gee, you have a beautiful smile." Women certainly want to hear this, but at that point in the conversation it may come off as completely insincere, and she will assume you haven't been listening to a word she has said. The key here, fellows, is be sincere and know your timing when you compliment and it will be received that way.

Talking about the exes, we all know, is a big TURN-OFF! If you need further explanation (although we can't imagine why), here it is. Your ex has nothing to do with your date and is, we hope, part of your past. She doesn't care about your ex nor is she interested in changing the circumstances relating to your ex. This topic is something to discuss in therapy and she is NOT your therapist. If you have unresolved issues surrounding your prior relationship, we advise you to seek a professional before you start dating again.

One last note, again, don't use foul language for any reason, please!

Cell Phones, PDA's, Other Communication Devices

Unless you have an emergency, don't even think about it! It's flat out rude to talk on the phone when you are spending time with someone. We're sure you wouldn't like it if they did it to you. If you don't believe us, check out the expressions on the girls faces on the cover of this book! That's exactly the expression you'll get from Jane, if you're that rude. If you have children and you need to leave it on in case of an emergency, put it on vibrate. If it rings and it's one of your children or the babysitter, answer and briefly find out what the issue is. If it's not an emergency, wrap it up as quickly as possible. No other calls should ever be answered for any reason whatsoever. That's why there is voicemail.

> **"Confidence is the number one attribute Jane finds most attractive about Jack!"**

How to Read the Signs on the Date
She's not into you?

Sometimes this is a little tricky. Chemistry, oh that chemistry, how do we explain this? Let's try a scenario. You've decided to take her to a concert. Read her body language. Some tell tale signs that she's not into you may be that she will have a tendency to focus on the performance rather than making a lot of eye contact with you. She will lean away from you, appear to keep her distance and even fold her arms (as in avoiding any contact with you). This is not a good sign. Also, if you find after the concert on the way home, there isn't much in the way of conversation and there are long periods of silence, you may want to consider taking her home rather than trying to extend the date.

Note: You need to see things for what they really are and not what you want them to be, Jack!

She is into you?

Usually when there is chemistry and interest, she will smile endlessly. She will lean into you during conversations, she will glance at you often, and there will be lots of eye contact. She will forget that anyone else is around. There will be lots of flirting. She may stroke her hair, giggle, laugh at all your jokes, bat her eyelashes and perhaps even touch your arm affectionately. Yes, girls still flirt this way; however, **this does not mean that she's ready to jump into bed with you, Jack!**

What to Say When the Date Ends

Scenario A – If you don't want a second date

You have established that there is no connection. So, how do you tactfully end the date knowing you don't want to see her again? In all cases, you want to be a gentleman, which means being honest and not cruel. We are going to give you one fool proof "out" that you can use in any of these situations. Here it is: "It has been such a nice time and you are such a nice woman/person and it was a pleasure meeting you. Have a good day/night." Period! And, we mean,

Period! Don't elaborate, don't tell her you will call, just walk away!

Scenario B – If you want a second date

Hopefully, you have read the signs that we talked about earlier. So, we are going to assume that she too wants a second date. Fantastic! Now, don't screw it up! This opportunity will not come again! Few men understand the importance of asking for the second date on the first date. It shows interest and confidence. Here, again, we will give you a fool proof phrase that should work every time. "I have had such a wonderful time and I hope you did too. I would really like to see you again, what day are you available next week?" Hopefully, she will give you that information. If she has to check her schedule that's okay too, don't be discouraged she may just have a busy schedule. In either case, you then tell her "I will call you Monday or Tuesday to make definite plans." IMPORTANT: **Call when you say you are going to call!**

The Good Night Kiss

Don't try to kiss a girl good night whom you know is NOT into you! Just don't do it!

If she is into you, a short and sweet kiss is appropriate assuming she appears receptive to being kissed. NOT a slobbering, tongue twirling, mouth bath! Again, make sure you're correctly reading the signs. If she seems in a rush to get out of the car or get into her house and suddenly appears tense, then, even if you had a good time, save the kiss for the next date. Some women just feel uncomfortable kissing on the first date. It has nothing to do with whether she likes you or not. If she hesitates at the door and is facing you expectantly, go for it! The first kiss, for a woman, is extremely important! So if it doesn't feel right, don't rush it because it could literally kill the date and any chance for a second one.

Sex on the First Date, Yes or No?

This is just our opinion, but we do not recommend that sex be a part of the first date. We, of course, live in the 21st century and understand that there are women who will have sex with you on a first date. But, because we want you to be successful and move it on to the second date, we suggest waiting. This shows you have respect for her and she will appreciate that you did not even make the attempt. We hope that you are reading this because you want to be set apart from the rest and by being a gentleman on the first date, you will do that. Let's be honest, Jack, can we say that most of the women you have had sex with on the first date, you most likely did not call again? If you're really being honest with yourself you'll agree with us. You're decision in this matter should reflect whether you want to have a second date or a one night stand. Choose to be a gentleman!

For You, Jane

Three Times a Lady

Deciding what to wear, what to talk about, and what to order for dinner can create a lot of confusion and stress. Women tend to worry about their appearance and conduct more than men do. We've all read that you shouldn't order spaghetti on a first date because it can potentially lead to unattractive slurping. Most men, though, don't want to see a woman order a meal and eat 3 bites of it and say she is full, either. Given that, we have developed some useful strategies that should help you be yourself and alleviate the anxiety as well. Due to the differences in how the two genders date, this section is specifically tailored for you Jane.

What NOT to Wear – Seriously

Fashion says a lot about you and it is your chance to express who you are. Remember that whenever you are heading out the door. As the old saying goes "You never get a second chance to make a first impression." We are not talking about running up to the corner store or the gym. What we are talking about here, is an outing with the possibility, or intention, of trying to meet someone.

Clothing should always fit you properly and look good on you. Just because you see it in a magazine, doesn't mean it's suitable for your body type. Women who wear things that are too tight or too baggy do nothing to compliment their figure. A woman who wears clothes that look good and complement her figure will go further than a woman who only wears the latest fads no matter how they look on her. Here's our rule of thumb, when you want to dress in a sexy manner, show a little cleavage or show off your legs - NEVER both at the same time. You don't want to come across as trying too hard. Bottom line here girls, don't embarrass yourselves by showing off all of your goods from the start and leaving nothing to the imagination. Don't try to put on an outfit like you packed yourself into a sardine can. Too tight doesn't necessarily equate to being sexy. We recommend you own a good floor length mirror and you use it!

What TO Wear

A few staples in your closet should include an updated, good fitting pair of jeans, a stylish blouse, a nice sweater, and a pretty sundress. Of course, don't forget about that little black dress! This should cover most dating scenarios. As far as accessories, add some earrings, a ring or two, bracelet, and a necklace. We have heard men say, less is more feminine when it comes to jewelry so remember to keep it as an accessory and not as the focal point of the outfit. Let your personality and sense of style show through your choice of apparel. If you don't trust yourself, ask a girlfriend who you think has a sense of style. Shoes, oh how we love our shoes! Flats are made for walking, heals are made for being sexy. Do a little something sexy with your shoes. Now, we understand that some outings require you to do considerable walking, so we don't expect you to wear 4" heels. But a cute sandal with a 1 ½" to 2" heel will go a long way in finishing your look. And, ladies, men love legs and sexy shoes!

Do something with your hair. Understated is usually better when it comes to hair styles. Even if you aren't great at styling your own hair, there are some fantastic cuts that allow for little fussing and will still look good. Take it from our professional stylist, Angela, talk to your hairstylist for a few tips on what looks good on you for your hair type. Be open to their suggestions and try something new! A new hair style can make you feel so good. As she always says at the salon: "If you can't change your life, you can always change your hair."

Learning the Art of a Seductive Walk and Body Language

Every woman should know how to make a grand entrance, one that will get you positively noticed. It's mostly in the walk. Men have said "did you see the way she walks? Wow!" This is where women have the advantage. Men can't do this, ladies, so listen up! First, you must have good posture, no slouching or shuffling of your feet. Hold your head high, shoulders back, and tighten your core muscles (i.e., stomach). Don't swing

BABY, I'M FOR REAL

your arms like you're going for a power walk. Keep them loosely at your sides. Now, here's the trick, its all in the hips. When you slightly sway your hips from side to side as you walk, men see this as pure seduction. Practice at home in front of a mirror to make sure you are being subtle and not over-accentuating the hip movement. You want to sway, not shake! When you are approaching your date make eye contact accompanied with a big warm smile! They will not be able to resist this combination!

Body language speaks louder than words! If you are paying attention, you can read the language loud and clear. If a man or a woman is not into you, they will sit back in the chair, shoulders pulled back, arms crossed, which indicates they are trying to put distance between you. If they are into you, they will be leaning forward, with constant eye contact and arms open, which indicates that they're inviting you into their space. Please pay attention to the signs you are receiving as well as giving.

A quick tip, be sure not to over-accentuate hand and arm movements while conversing. Your date will feel insecure that you will either smack them accidentally or worse, knock over the drinks on the table. This can appear as if you are out of control and unsophisticated. If you find this difficult to do, we suggest that you place one hand in your lap with the other forearm draped loosely on the table. The best way to ensure you are sending the right message is to be aware of what your body is saying!

"Men dislike women who are angry and shout!"

How You Should Expect to be Treated

With respect in every way, period! This to us is a very important subject. Women should never allow anyone to disrespect them, but they do, and why is that? Without being psychologists, we can only give our opinions. We feel that when women feel insecure due to a recent breakup (perhaps one where they were not treated respectfully) or they don't feel confident, they will have a tendency to overlook bad behavior and perpetuate this cycle of abuse. Women need to break this cycle! If necessary, there is plenty of professional help out there or, at the very least, seek out a support system of friends and family. We also strongly recommend that after any significant break up, that you take time out to grieve and strengthen your self-esteem and self-worth. If you don't do this through gaining some independence, you may continue to jump into relationships that are unhealthy for you. If you feel independent and confident you are less likely to accept poor behavior. Listen up ladies, you deserve better! So, pull up your boot straps and be a warrior for your own independence and don't settle for less than you deserve!

Having said all of that, let's look at some examples of what to look for. Okay, ladies, if a man immediately uses foul language in front of you, see this as a red flag. Chances are this kind of disrespect will only get worse. We recognize that this use of foul language has been accepted in society, although, neither of us can understand why that is! We, however, still feel that a lady should be treated like a lady and, unless you are walking through the men's locker room, you should not have to accept hearing that kind of language and most certainly not on the first few dates. We recommend you speak up and tell them, in your own creative way, that you don't care to hear that sort of language. If they persist, kick them to the curb because they obviously don't care how you feel and you don't want someone who doesn't care! Next, if a man talks to you in a condescending manner, run for the hills and we mean leave skid marks! This is a form of emotional abuse and should never be tolerated! Also, watch carefully and see how they treat those that are in the service industry. If they are rude or mean to a waiter, for example, it will only be a matter of time before he turns it on you. We hope that by giving these few examples, we are helping to open your eyes in the early stages of dating because it's a lot easier to walk away early on.

No, You Should Not Have to Pay on the First Date

It's the first date, ladies, your man should pay. Now, down the road, if things are going well and you'd like to pick up the tab, that would be very nice and it would be appreciated. If you cannot afford it, then invite them over for dinner. Be sure that you both understand where you are at on the intimacy subject. Men have a tendency to assume when you invite them for dinner that it will turn into a slumber party. So be sure, if you don't want to have a sleep over, that you set those ground rules.

The Art of Conversation

There is nothing like great communication to keep the ball rolling, especially, when it's exciting and fun. Note here, two major conversation killers are: (1) talking about your exes and (2) talking too much about your children. First, they don't care about what your ex did or didn't do! They are not your therapist so don't treat them as such. Just don't do it! Next, your children are wonderful to you and "they do the cutest things," but quite frankly it's boring to your date especially if they have never met them. Now, we aren't saying you can't bring them up and share a couple of stories, but, please, keep them brief and move on to a conversation that you both can share in. If you both find it fascinating to talk about children because you both have them, fabulous, but don't assume everyone feels the same about your kids as you do. There are plenty of subjects that you can find to talk about that interest both of you. If you aren't sure how to start a conversation, simply ask "what are your interests?" This should generate enough to get through an evening.

Men don't care for jabber jaws. You do have to give them a chance to talk as well. They say that women are born communicators and, well, women do love to talk a subject to death. Here is a tip: there is nothing like beating a dead horse… with your girlfriends! Your date is not your girlfriend. If you see his eyes start to glaze over or you have forgotten what his voice sounds like, you are probably dominating too much of the conversation.

Cell Phones, PDA's and other Communication Devices

As for Jack, the same for Jane! Unless you have an emergency, don't even think about it! It's flat out rude to talk on the phone when you are spending time with someone and I'm sure you wouldn't like it if they did it to you. If you don't believe us, check out the expressions on the girls' faces on the cover of this book! That's exactly the expression you'll get from Jack, if you're that rude. If you have children and you need to leave it on in case of an emergency, put it on vibrate. If it rings and it's one of your children or the babysitter, answer it and briefly find out what the issue is. If it's not an emergency, wrap it up as quickly as possible. No other calls should ever be answered for any reason whatsoever. That's why there is voicemail.

"Ladies, did you know that touching your hair at any time is flirty and sexy?"

How to Read the Signs

He's not into you!

Women generally have fairly good instincts when it comes to reading signs of interest. For those of you that still get a little stumped, we offer these few pointers to help you out. Let's talk about body language. How many times have you seen guys with their hands in their pockets like they're glued in there or their arms look like a padlock across their chest? This isn't a good sign. It's definitely a means of keeping you at a distance. If it seems to loosen up as the date progresses, you may be okay and it could have been first date nerves. If, however, he pretty much keeps his hands to himself the entire evening, this will probably be the first and last date. The other big sign is lack of eye contact and keeping their answers short in response to your attempt at conversing. This too should also be looked at as a sign that it will be a one date wonder. Try not to be disappointed, as there just isn't any connection and better to find out early so you don't get emotionally attached. There is plenty of fish in the sea and you should see it as an opportunity to be free to move on so you can find the right catch for you.

He is into you!

He's one lucky Jack! If a man is into you, sister, you will know it! A bomb could go off right next to him, and he'd still only have eyes for you! They will usually find any reason to be near you and find a reason to touch you (and we don't mean in a sexual manner). For example, he may touch your hand, help you with your coat and move your hair, and perhaps put his hand on your leg. If he's a true gentleman he'll walk you to your car, open your car door, or walk you to your front door to ensure your safety. These are all very good signs that he's intrigued.

What to Say When the Date Ends

You don't want to see him again

Okay, you just don't want to hurt someone's feelings, but, for your sake as well as his, be gently honest if he asks for a second date. Don't lead someone on because you don't know how to say "no thank you." We know this is difficult, we have been there too. Here is an easy out: "I really had a nice time and thank you for everything, but I just don't feel the connection." Don't say anything more! Women often think the more they say, the softer the blow, but, actually, less is more in this situation. If you're in the car, get out! If you're at the front door, go in! BE STRONG, HAVE COURAGE! You will feel better if you handle it in this manner rather than the alternative, which is feeling guilty every time he calls while you try to dodge him.

You do want to see him again

Let's assume you both would like to see each other again. If he doesn't ask you out right then for a second date, you could encourage him by saying, "this was so much fun! We should do this again." That lets him know in no uncertain terms that you are interested. He will then feel more confident in asking you out at that moment or calling you soon for a second date. Nobody likes to be rejected, so it's up to you to let him know that he won't be.

The Good Night Kiss

Let him lead the first kiss. You don't want to force an uncomfortable situation for either of you. Believe us, if he's into you, he'll want to kiss you. If he is not into you, he won't initiate a first kiss and just leave it at that. If he tries to initiate a kiss and you feel uncomfortable with that, no matter the reason, you are under no obligation to kiss him. Even if you have a great time, you can save it for another date. If he initiates a kiss and you are receptive to being kissed, you go girl! Hopefully, he will have read the signs and it will be a short and sweet kiss and not a "slobbering, tongue twirling mouth bath." As Rhett Butler (from the movie *Gone with the Wind* for you young ones who don't know who Rhett Butler is) would say "You need to be kissed often and by someone who knows how to!"

Sex on the First Date, Yes or No

You are totally in control of this situation. You do not have to have sex on a first date if you don't want to. Women, in this country, have the upper hand when it comes to this topic. If it is initiated it will or will not occur based on your decision. Now, our opinion on this subject is to leave this for another time. We do not recommend you have sex on the first date, unless you never want to see him again. If you want to see this relationship progress, however, then we say "sit tight" baby! Give it some time. There is a lot to be said for getting to know someone first. You will gain his respect and, more importantly, you will maintain your own self-respect. There is nothing more important than that!

CHAPTER 7

The Tears of a Clown

Sometimes you can play your music so loud that even ear plugs can't muffle the noise. There are just some forms of music that should be softer in tone. Below are several reasons why your date may have chosen to dance to a different tune.

1. No Chemistry

This will kill a relationship faster than applying too much weed and feed to your lawn. What can we say, it's either there or its not! You can't take it personally if someone just doesn't feel it for you. You shouldn't feel guilty when you don't feel it for them, either. Don't lead them on

THE TEARS OF A CLOWN

by accepting another date when you both could be moving on to find someone you have a mutual attraction for.

2. Dressed Trashy / Sloppily for a First Date

Nothing is worse than meeting someone for the first time who looks like a complete train wreck. Please guys, no stains, rips, vulgar T-shirts, tennis shoes (unless you're going to the gym), and baseball caps for a first date! If you're trying to hide the fact that you don't have hair under that baseball cap, be warned that it just isn't going to protect you for long, there, Junior. Either a girl likes you or she doesn't (with or without hair, it shouldn't matter).

Ladies, ladies, ladies, it's great to wear a short skirt, but if it's so short that when you sneeze you expose more than a little leg, we might offer the tip that it's too short. As the saying goes "if you've got it flaunt it" but let's not get too carried away on that first date and show him all your stuff! A little left to the imagination can go a long way and keeps them coming back for more. As for that luscious cleavage you may so luckily have been endowed with, leave your "girls" under wraps for a little while at least. Men can appreciate your curves through your clothing, trust us. You will send the wrong message and we want those men to get the right message loud and clear!

"Did you know that asking too many personal questions initially is a turn off?"

3. Ignore Them Like They Are a Statue with No Name

This is a good way to never get a call back. Think about it, if you were so busy looking around the room at all the other men and women like you were a kid in a candy store with too much to choose from, how do you think your date would feel? If you are preoccupied with work or some other big issue, you should consider rescheduling for a time when you feel more emotionally available. Otherwise, you should understand why in three days you haven't heard anything from them. It's exhausting when you feel like you are the only one on the date. Most men or women in this scenario would rather sit at home and watch a movie alone.

4. Negative Attitude

This is just the worst! Trying to have a conversation with someone whose every reply is negative, or they are a naysayer, is just too much work! UGGG! These people have an ugly outlook on life and don't have a nice thing to say about anyone or anything. If you are one of these kinds of people, we can almost guarantee that you will never get a call back. You people with this attitude, drain our energy and suck the life out of the rest of us and we don't want to spend another moment with you! Seriously! Put that negativity away and find something, anything, to be positive about. And, for you folks who make fun of others or say derogatory statements about every race or culture, stay home with your bad self because we just plain don't like you!

5. Two Different Intellectual Levels

A call back may not happen if your idea of an intellectual topic of conversation is "why they don't have a comic strip section in the Wall Street Journal" and your date's is "how the financial market is affecting today's economic climate." You might be on two very different levels intellectually. We're not saying that this can't work, but this type of disparity can be frustrating for both parties. If you don't get a call back, again, don't take this personally. You may simply not have the same views as they do and you both should be looking for someone more in your intellectual arena.

6. More Time on the Phone with Your Friends than Talking to Them

It's amazing that we even have to address this issue, but we think you'd be surprised at how often this happens. It's funny to you to get text messages from your friends while on a date, but it's not so fun for the person sitting across from you who's left out of the joke! Put the phone away! We are going to say it again, PUT THE PHONE AWAY! Your friends and family can live without hearing back from you for an hour or two. Your rudeness will find you more times than not, without a second date!

7. Just Plain Boring

Most people would prefer to be on their couch with a good book than spend 30 minutes with a person who has nothing of interest to say. If you are extremely shy and quiet and find yourself with little to talk about, we suggest you brush up on your conversation skills prior to getting into the dating world. If you find it difficult to talk about yourself then we suggest you get on line and (1) read a couple of current news articles, (2) look up the latest movies that are out, or (3) discuss your favorite vacation destinations, etc. Please, just talk about something, anything, that strikes your fancy (obviously, be tasteful and within reason). Communication is the key to any relationship. If you can't contribute in any way, you certainly will not receive a call back. You have to find a way to stand on that leg no matter how wobbly it may be.

8. Acting like a Child

Most of us at this point have given up babysitting our younger siblings or the neighbor kids and we certainly aren't interested in babysitting you! If you're going to behave like a child, expect that you will not get a return call from any reasonable adult looking for an adult relationship. So, grow up, if you want to continue to date.

9. Got Sloppy Drunk

Trust us, this is really not attractive. When you embarrass someone by getting drunk and becoming loud and obnoxious, you'll be lucky if they don't leave you at the bar, let alone ever hear from them again. This is not only humiliating for you and your date, it can make your date feel as though you put them in a dangerous situation! Especially, if you have a tendency to pick fights or get confrontational with people when you drink. Learn to control yourself or you will be love's big loser!

10. You're Manners Challenged

When your date can count the hairs on your half bald head because you're eating like you're at a pig's trough, you might be manners challenged. If this is the case, we recommend you get on line and find a crash course on manners before you make a complete fool of yourself. Shoveling food in your mouth and talking with your mouth open is so unattractive you may find they disappear through the bathroom window. Now, if you find you are overzealous in your physical gestures, such as slapping your date in the arm as you loudly laugh, you may find that your date won't see the humor in discovering a bruise on their bicep. I'm sure when they set out for the evening; they weren't thinking they were going to be signing up for a boxing match. This will pretty much ensure they will move on to a more non-violent person in the future. Do us all a favor and keep your hands to yourself!

11. You've set the Wrong Expectations

If you have portrayed yourself to be something that you're not or you are living in the past, which doesn't resemble who you are currently, your date will most likely be disappointed and feel misled. Is it necessary for us to give you an explanation as to why they wouldn't call you back? Be honest about who you are now, not who you were (or who you want to be) because your date is going to see you in the present. Be real, it's not as bad as you think!

> "Laughter is good for the soul, so be generous with your laughter!"

12. Too Pushy

So, let's say you had a great first date and they seem to like you and you liked them. Instead of taking it slow, you start calling and text messaging them constantly every day since the first date. This can be overwhelming and the person whose attention you so desperately are seeking will most likely run like the wind. This has the M.O. of the beginning stages of being a stalker and even though you may not be one, all that will matter is that you will come across like one. So, take a breath and let nature take its course. You can be attentive without being aggressive. If they do not call you back after the first message, leaving 20 messages isn't going to help you.

13. The Lethal Injection

So, you had sex on the first date, now what? You hope and pray that they call you back. Well, if they do, it's rare and it's usually because you left something at their house. As a rule, this is not the most ideal way to get a second date. Most of us have figured out that if you are willing to sleep with them on the first date, then you have slept with others on the first date as well. They will not consider you to be a person they will want a relationship with. This goes for both men and women. So, unless you're looking for the ultimate date killer, we suggest you refrain and save the sex for down the road.

CHAPTER 8

Baby, I Need Your Lovin'

Keep your ego in check! Just because you've made it through the first date, doesn't mean your song is complete! There is still a lot of music left to write. If you follow the next step, provided in this section, you will continue to keep on track and get closer to becoming a star. So, head back to your recording studio and keep on creating.

For You, Jack

My Girl

You are now listening to the same music and, if played correctly, could very well lead to dancing in the streets. Your next few dates will help you establish whether this is going to be a long term recording contract or a one hit wonder. You can continue to set yourself apart during your courtship if you follow some of these very simple rules designed specifically for you.

It's All About a Plan A . . . and B

Let's start with Plan A. We know you guys have busy schedules, so do us women! Please call by Wednesday for a Saturday night date! This shows your intentions are admirable and you are interested. Don't call Friday night after you've made sure that you have nothing better to do. Guess what, women know that's what you're doing. You're not fooling anyone and they don't deserve to be second best to your buddies, sporting events, or other more interesting lady friends. Now that we have cleared up this matter for you, DON'T INSULT THEM BY TRYING IT!

Okay, back to Plan A. When you call on Wednesday, please make solid, firm plans. Go ahead and assume that she is going to accept your offer of a date, so make sure that you are prepared in advance. Don't say "okay, well, I'll call you later to set something up." Set it up then! Nothing is more frustrating than putting their Saturday on hold waiting for you to grace them with a call. Be sure to let her know where you are going so she knows how to dress, especially, if it's a special event. If you are going somewhere you haven't been before, do a little pre-planning research. You need to know where you are go-ing, what the dress code is and how to get there. There are plenty of avenues to do this type of research. If you do not have access to the Internet, then ask around for suggestions on places to go, or look in the Yellow Pages and call the establishment. It's even okay to ask her if there is a particular place she likes to go, if you are unfa-miliar with the area. Be sure to get directions!

Always make sure to have a Plan B in place. Do we need to say more?

All of these tips will set you apart from other men and will score you points for future dates and isn't that what we are trying to accomplish? Getting to the sec-ond date, at least?

Spontaneous Activities

These are what we fondly call "fillers." For example, you get tickets to a sporting event or a concert at the last minute. Feel free to call and see if she is available.

Now this is not to be confused with an actual planned date. Remember, these are infrequent and spontaneous. Don't get caught up in thinking that you can do this on a regular basis, at least not for the few first dates. If you do this too often, it comes off like you are waiting to ensure something better (or someone better), doesn't come along. You're obviously not making her a priority.

Setting an Appropriate Pace

This is a tough subject simply because relationships will take on their own personality. Be warned, if it is really hot to begin with, it can fizzle out just as quickly. Think of it like a roaring fire that suddenly doesn't have enough wood or oxygen to sustain it for a long time. What you want is to start with slow burning embers and let it build by constantly adding the fuel that makes it turn to flames.

Typically, setting two dates per week (once during the week and once on the weekend) is a good beginning pace. Include a couple of phone calls or emails to keep the communication on going. This shows you have a definite interest, but are not overwhelming her, which could scare her off. If, down the road, things seem to be progressing, then you will get a feel for how much time you can spend with each other and the pace will pick up speed naturally.

> "Some things are worth waiting for, like the first kiss!"

When to Stop the Pursuit

You have both agreed to a second date and she goes MIA (missing in action). You have left a couple telephone messages and an email and it's been at least two to three days since your last message and she has not responded. I'm sure just by reading that sentence you ought to be able to figure out that she's probably hiding from you. But you're thinking, maybe she's just really busy at work or something tragic has happened. I mean, what else could it be? We are sorry to be the bearer of bad news, but clearly she's dodging you and doesn't know how to tell you that she's not interested in furthering this friendship. We would suggest that you STOP! Don't go any further and move on.

What to Do if You Are Not into Her

You have been on two to three dates now and you are discovering that you're not feeling the love. What to do? We know it's really hard to hurt someone's feelings, but in the end it's the right thing to do no matter how much it stings. We will give you an "out" here that should work in most cases and should be done in a gentle manner. We recommend that you make a clean break. Telling someone that you "want to remain friends" can perpetuate hope on their part that something will develop later through that friendship, which is misleading. The following statement (or a variation thereof), is honest, yet to the point: "I really enjoyed getting to know you, but I don't think the connection for me is there. I wish you the best in your life and hope you find what you are looking for."

Putting In the Work

Okay, so at this point you have been on several dates. Does that mean that you can just sit back on your laurels and stop doing any of the work? A big fat NO! Relationships are work from start to finish (in other words "till death do you part"). When the passion and freshness of a new relationship comes to a halt and complacency takes over you are now in danger of the relationship breaking down. The distance between you will widen so far that you will completely lose sight of each other. Work, work, work! We know that doesn't sound like fun, but if you take the advice of some very insightful dwarfs and "whistle while you work," you could turn work into play and downright enjoy yourself!

Think of it this way, if you are doing a household project yourself (e.g., adding an addition to the house or finishing off a basement), it takes work, right? When it's complete, though, you feel so proud of what you have accomplished because it was something that you put your time and energy into. It turned out so beautiful and now you want to share it with the world. That's the same as a relationship. If you continue to put the time and effort into it, it will also turn out to be something you can feel very proud of.

Now, we are not only talking about single people here. You married folks, or those thinking of getting married, must always remember: dating is a lifetime event. As our friend, Dr. Terry Lyles said in the Forward of our book "Couples need the same insight to maintain a healthy and vibrant loving relationship and the key to longevity with another person is keeping it fresh." We think this is the golden rule to maintain any solid, loving relationship.

Courting Should Continue

Think back to the first couple of dates that you went on. The energy level, anticipation, and excitement should not fade in the first three months. This is not necessarily a time that you should feel that you have to spend every day together, but you should continue to consistently date at least 2-3 times a week. Obviously you need to keep the communication going, so you can feel free to call, email, text (whatever) regularly. This also means that you should continue to keep the romance alive (e.g., sending cards, flowers, token gifts, romantic meals, well you should be getting the picture). Depending on where you are at intimately with each other, a romantic getaway isn't out of the question during this time. We understand that dating can be expensive, so if you need to watch your expenses, then you may have to be a bit more creative. We would suggest a morning movie (which is usually less expensive than the evening shows). Using a little common sense and creativity can go a long way.

Keep Calling / Stay in Touch

Communication is key in developing a strong, healthy, and meaningful dating experience or relationship. If you do not keep in touch regularly throughout the first three months, the object of your affection will most likely lose interest quickly. If you like this person, stay in the game! Just a tip, we know that you all love your cell phones; however, be careful that you don't get too caught up in the text messages. They can be fun and flirty, but impersonal if this is your only means of communicating between dates. Hearing a voice and having more in-depth conversation helps you get to know someone better and will deepen the relationship.

Stay on Your Best Behavior

It's easy to fall into a comfort zone and get too sloppy. During the first three months, you should still be careful about what you say in terms of foul language and distasteful topics of conversation. There is nothing more unattractive than a man who can't seem to find anything else to talk about other than sex. There are so many other things to discuss that are far more interesting to women and will make you look like an intelligent, tasteful, gentleman.

Continue to Dress for Success

We don't expect you to show up in a suit for every date, but make sure that your clothes are appropriate for the occasion. They should be clean, in good shape, tasteful and up-to-date. Please don't <u>ever</u> show up with a Tee Shirt that has some offensive or derogatory statement about women or sex (e.g., "I had sex with your sister."). Continuing to put effort into your appearance shows your enthusiasm and continued interest in the relationship.

Don't Give up all of Your Friends

We understand that meeting a new girl that you are wild about is fun and exciting and you want to initially spend every minute together. However, finding balance in your life is extremely important, even in the very early stages of a relationship. You never want to lose your identity and if you feel that the woman you are seeing expects you to drop everyone for her, this should be a big warning sign. There is nothing worse than feeling like you can't breathe in a relationship. Here's a great example: if you cannot go out golfing for a few hours without her text messaging or calling you constantly, you ought to consider "slicing" her from your life. Just as the golf ball sometimes gets lost in the rough, so should she get lost. Come on guys, this doesn't mean she cares, this means she's controlling and, yes, just as you suspect, is checking up on you!

On the flip side, we don't mean hanging out with your friends every Friday night, golfing every Saturday, and working on your buddy's hotrod every Sunday. What we mean is that you keep in touch with your buds and get together occasionally and she should be doing the same with her girlfriends. As they say, absence makes the heart grow fonder. Not to mention that it is less likely you will both feel smothered, which can ruin a good thing very quickly. Balance, balance, balance!

> "Did you know that dancing is a
> physical contact sport, so just do it!"

Don't Give up your Family, Especially Your own Children

We know that there are certain family obligations that we all have to tend to. If you are very family oriented, it would be wise of you to consider any woman that you get involved with also be family oriented. For one thing, she will understand more of those responsibilities and be willing to go along with them. More importantly, if you have children, we also recommend that you express very clearly the place they have in your life. If she wants to be a big part of your life as well, she should be willing to include them in hers. NEVER give up your children or your family for anyone! If they are the right one, they won't ask you to. Choose wisely!

Keeping Your own Interests Intact

Each of us is an individual and we should all relish in that fact. We all have individual goals, dreams and desires in life. If someone is really interested in you, they would encourage you to pursue your dreams and not feel threatened by them. Never let the balloon of dreams be popped by someone else. Compatibility is important, but it's unrealistic to think that you should have everything in common. It is simply impossible because women and men are so different. You should have several things that you enjoy doing together. There is nothing wrong, though, with having your own interests that the other doesn't share as long as those interests don't consume you and you end up losing sight of the relationship.

Listen to Your Friends

This one is near and dear to our hearts and one of the most difficult things to do. We never like to hear the negative comments about our love interests from our friends, even when we know they are right. Here is the key. Only listen to those friends whom you feel you can trust and you believe fully that they have your best interest at heart. If you feel that your friend is trying to sabotage your relationship out of jealousy or because you are not as available, then we caution you to consider what their motives may be. If, though, a friend you trust points out certain negative behavior patterns they see in this person, it would behoove you to at least step back and take a reality check. Remember that it's always easier to look from the outside in, especially, when your emotions can block the view.

You are Responsible for Your own Life and Happiness!

Where does it say that your happiness lies in the hands of someone else? If you're not happy, we don't care who you meet, they will NOT make you happy. You may feel the temporary euphoria of meeting and seeing a new and exciting woman, but ultimately, you will be disappointed when you rely on them for your happiness. As you came into this world alone, you will leave it alone too. The only thing a significant other can do is to enhance your happiness. True happiness lies within you and cannot be found through other people or things. If you rely on others to make you happy you will be forever disappointed because no one has the answers for you. It's simply said in one word: Peace. If you have that, happiness will follow naturally.

Don't be a Chameleon

If you are sitting at the opera, feeling the blood pouring out of your ears from the piercing vocals of the woman singing on stage wondering why in the heck they sing the words instead of just talking, odds are you have mislead your lady friend. Okay, so you gave it a try and you hate it, there is no shame in that. The trick is to be honest about it. If this happens to be a deal breaker, well, then you may want to check it off as this is not the right girl for you. We all want to make a good impression and there is nothing wrong with trying new things. When you try to change your life and interests, however, in order to convince her that she is right for you, we can pretty much guarantee that it will not work. Eventually, you will begin to resent her for "making" you do things you don't like and it will cause conflict and most likely end the relationship.

Building and Maintaining Respect

Aretha Franklin sings, "R E S P E C T, find out what it means to me!" It means the same to all of us. We all want and deserve respect and consideration. It's not as hard as you think. Respect is simply caring enough about another person to want to encourage and not demoralize. For those of you who need a little help understanding, here are a few examples. Let's say you're at a party with mixed company and you start to cuss like a Neanderthal. This is disrespectful, not only to the woman you're with, but to all of the women in the group. Most women do not care for that kind of language and we hope that you are smart enough to be able to come up with different adjectives to express your views. Or, worse, you share some embarrassing story with the group about your girl that was meant to be private and laugh at her expense. Not only does it humiliate her, but makes you look like a complete jerk for telling the story. Remember, you're with her! One last example would be raising your voice at her in a public place over some trivial matter and humiliate her in front of a bunch of strangers. This is NOT the time and place to have an argument of any kind. Trust us when we say that most likely people will feel sorry for her that she's with you and you will look like the idiot.

We know that we are coming off very strong sounding on this subject because we feel it is so important. So, getting back to the lighter side, think of how your heart goes pitter patter when you look at your "baby" (e.g., your Harley Davidson motorcycle or your 1970 mint condition Chevy . . . you get the picture). So, what do you do? You make sure she's oiled, buffed, shining and has the best accessories money can buy. We know you even talk lovingly as you're covering her up for the night "sweet dreams baby." Okay, Jack, if you can treat your girl like you do your "baby," then . . . . well, trust us it will be REALLY good!

Start a Tradition between the Two of You

Relationships are private between two people and tradition bonds people together. So, if you start something that becomes a memory that only you two share, it will start a bond that can last a lifetime.

Think of chiseling something into stone rather than writing in sand, which can be washed away with the evening tide. Memories will always be with you no matter what. If you have fond memories with each other it only continues to build on a healthy, loving, long-lasting relationship. For those of you who think, "I wonder what they mean by this," here are a couple of examples of the do's and don'ts. Throwing her into the pool at the annual family reunion may be funny to you, but not necessarily a fond memory for her. Well, unless she has an incredible sense of humor. This we still think is a "don't." A couple of do's would be, every year on Memorial Day weekend you go to the same place (e.g., bed and breakfast, outdoor fair, or any kind of fun adventure that the two of you would enjoy together). Another tradition could be finding a favorite dessert place that you go to every Sunday evening (and, by the way fellows, we don't mean the one behind closed doors). Use your own creativity to spark something that is original and meaningful to both of you.

Include Her in Your Life

What we are talking about here is bringing her into your circle of friends and family. There is nothing worse than being involved with someone who makes you feel like you are an outsider. If she is going to be a part of your life then she should be involved in most of your activities. Having said that, we know that the issue of meeting family and friends is a tough one. Some people feel that it's a sign of commitment when you introduce someone you're dating to your family or friends, while others don't feel as strongly about this. We would say that it's up to you to decide when it's appropriate based on your individual relationship and your relationship with your family and friends.

On a side note: if by chance you and she have not established that you are exclusive, you may want to consider informing your buddies beforehand to zip their lips to avoid any hurt feelings or embarrassment.

For You, Jane

My Guy

Listening to the beat of two drums in unison can be exhilarating! However, listening to the beat of your own drum is also very important. First things first, don't sit by the phone waiting for him to call and don't call him. Go about the business of living your life. A man will call if they are interested, we promise! When he does call for that second, third, and fourth date (and beyond), here are some helpful hints on what to expect and what he should expect from you.

When to Accept a Second Date

The rule of thumb is you never accept a date after Wednesday for the up-coming weekend. The most ideal situation is he makes a plan for a second date with you on the first date. However, that isn't always the case. So, if he leaves it open, then he should call you by Wednesday. Now, ladies, this does not mean he calls you Wednesday, chats on the phone and says "what are you doing this weekend?" You say "I don't have that much going on." And, he says "well, I'll call you later and we'll set something up!" Seriously, this means "let me make sure that nothing better comes along before I make a solid plan with you!" We don't know about you, but we think this is just plain rude, unacceptable, and disrespectful. We don't believe this guy is really that into you! You deserve better. You deserve to have someone who thinks you're worth their time and effort, because you are. Even if you have nothing to do, better to call a friend or read a book than be second or third choice down the list of things he wants to do.

> **"Did you know that Jack doesn't want to hear about men from your past?"**

Spontaneous Activities

Now, there are only a couple of exceptions to the rule! If, for example, he calls because he received last minute tickets for a sporting event or a concert, feel free to accept. As long as he is not making a habit of "last minute deals" we think you're okay to go along for the fun, if you are available. We do not, however, recommend that you break previously made plans to go on a last minute date. Don't ever blow off your girlfriends just to go out with a guy. Believe us Jane, he won't drop his plans for you. You are entitled to have a life outside of your dating and don't ever deny yourself that for the sake of getting a date.

Setting an Appropriate Pace

In the beginning stages of dating you should expect to hear from him a couple of times a week, whether by email or telephone. He should be setting at least one to two dates per week. If he's calling all that time, wanting to see you every day and you feel a little overwhelmed, you may need to slow things down. You can do that by simply not being available every time he calls.

Keeping Those Rose Colored Glasses OFF

See things as they REALLY are and not as you would want them to be. You have to be able to see warning signs very early in the dating process, long before you allow your emotions to become involved. Let us give you an example or two. If he constantly calls or emails you, but never seems to make time to see you (i.e., work is crazy, kid issues, friends need him, fixing his house . . . we could go on and on), well we hate to tell you, but he's not into you. If he was, he'd make time for you, and that's the truth of it! You deserve to be a priority.

Okay, if the first one didn't open your eyes, how about this example. When you are together and he treats you disrespectfully, you justify it by saying "oh poor Jack, he's under just so much stress with his job . . . (or whatever it is)." Plain and simple, this is who he is and you will be treated this way no matter what is going on in his life. If you enjoy being second or third down the list or you don't mind that he takes his anger/frustration out on you, well, go for it. Personally, we think you deserve better and we hope you think so too!

Do Not Be the One to Pursue

This is a typical mistake a lot of today's women make. After the first date, they initiate emails or text messages, etc. We do not recommend that you do this in the early stages of dating. Men like the hunt and if you are too accessible, available, or even go so far as to take over the pursuit, you take the fun out of it for them. We know it can be tough to sit and wait for them to contact you, so don't sit around pining for them. Get busy doing your own thing and living your life. This is like boot camp girls, pull up your boot straps and become your own person. Men love confident women and if you have your own interests and hobbies, you will be much more interesting to them. We offer a suggestion. If you don't have any hobbies, then find something that touches your heart and volunteer your time. For example, if you love animals, the humane societies and endangered species organizations are always looking for volunteers. You'd be surprised at the number of organizations that help kids, animals, and the disenfranchised in general to whom you could offer your services. You will gain a greater sense of self-worth and you will find that most men will admire you for this. Volunteering is a very attractive quality. Also, this way if he decides to fly back to Mars and you never hear from him again, well, at least you didn't waste your time waiting on him. The added benefit is the knowledge that you have contributed to many gratifying causes and enhanced your life in the process.

What to Do If You Are Not into Him

Okay, ladies, we have all done the dodge ball routine. Those of us who have been in the singles scene for any length of time have run into this situation. If you're lucky, he will feel the same after the first date. If you are not so lucky and he doesn't give up on the pursuit, even after you have tried to dodge him, then you're going to have to face the music and speak up. Sometimes, it takes a hammer on the head to get the message across. The biggest complaint that men have is that we aren't up front and don't tell them what we want, so that's what we are going to do! Most men don't want to be just friends, so we recommend you stay away from the "let's just be friends" routine. We have been told that they would prefer you were flat out honest with them. So, be kind but firm. Here is an out you can use.

"I have enjoyed getting to know you, but the connection isn't there for me. I wish you the best in life and I hope you find what you are looking for."

How to Stay in the Present

Since you were little girls, you read many a fairytale and dreamed of a knight in shining armor coming to save you from the drudgery of everyday life. Then you grow up and have to face reality! Yet, you still fantasize about the wedding, marriage, babies, and the house with the white picket fence before you even get to the third date. You need to stay in the present and be real about your expectations. Don't fantasize too far into the future! This will prevent a lot of heartache and disappointment. Come on girls wake up! See things for what they really are. It is impossible for men to meet some of these huge expectations that we set for them. See them for the real flawed human beings that they are and use your head in making a sound decision about the person you see in front of you. The furthest thought into the future should be whether you want to go on another date.

"Did you know that the most approachable colors for women are pink and peach as it brings out a man's protective instincts?"

BABY, I NEED YOUR LOVIN'

Putting in the Work

At this point, you can start to feel free to initiate plans. Now, don't get too crazy with this and start planning everything. We know that a lot of women like to take over the schedule of events; however, we feel that you should continue to allow him to pursue you. Don't get ahead of yourself! You can, however, feel free to invite him to a barbecue at your house, write little love notes and send cards, or plan a special evening for the two of you. Or here is another idea that is cute, leave a message on their voicemail. There is nothing like coming home at the end of a long day to a sweet message. Everyone, including men, enjoy a little appreciation and attention.

Courting Should Continue

Enjoy the courting process. Don't be so quick to rush to the "relationship" part. The anticipation of a call or a date is half the fun, so don't be in such a hurry to become a "couple." Women by nature are nurturers and they have a tendency to want to help clean, organize, and feed the men in their lives. Please watch out for this tendency. Men can be very intimidated when a women steps in and wants to take control of their lives too soon. There is plenty of time to help with these chores later (**and we do mean later**) in the relationship. This is the time to get to know the person, not their cupboards, how they fold their towels, or what's on their grocery list. The work we are talking about is building your personal relationship with him, not work in the sense of actual labor. Remember to stop and smell the roses that, by the way, he should continue to be sending you.

Pushiness Does Not Become You

One of the biggest complaints we hear from men is dealing with a needy woman who calls him constantly. We know that everyone now has cell phones but that doesn't give you the right to constantly call or text message him. If he is busy at work or out on the golf course, you need to be respectful of his time away from you. Nothing is more irritating than a clingy, needy, "doesn't have their own life" kind of woman. There is something to be said for playing a little hard to get. Here is a little secret, don't always be so predictable or accessible. Men are natural born hunters, it's much more fun for them if you occasionally find a good hiding spot and let them work a little bit to find you. Never let him think he's totally got you. Leave them guessing once in a while. Believe us, if they truly care about you, they will love it! A play by play of your daily routine is boring and unnecessary.

On the flip side, if he is constantly calling or text messaging you wanting to know where you are and who you are with, this is not flattery, concern or caring, it's control. Yes, as you suspect, it's a form of checking up on you. We suggest you don't accept this behavior. If you are the one checking up on him, you as well are being controlling and he should find it unacceptable. You have the right (as does he) to enjoy outside interests without having to check in or answer to him. Have a little self respect, ladies!

Stay on Your Best Behavior

We know that all those cute little stories of how your guy got lost going to the concert are fun for you to tell in public; however, please realize that men usually find those cute stories to be embarrassing and demoralizing. Please be careful not to bruise their ego, especially, among their friends and co-workers. Another fatal mistake is bringing up an ex-boyfriend or husband, which may seem harmless to you, but no one really likes to hear about your prior relationships, especially, your new guy. If you are comparing them in any way, it makes you sound as though you still have feelings for the ex. If you do, we suggest you deal with those feelings before you get back in the dating scene! This is a big turn off to most men, so just don't do it!

Also, a side note here, if you're one of those girls who likes to curse, please be sure to gargle with Lysol before you leave the house. Truly ladies this is not attractive or lady-like and we would highly recommend that you buy yourself a dictionary and learn other adjectives to use as we know you are much smarter than that.

Continue to Dress for Success

It's easy to fall into a comfort zone and get a little too sloppy. Now, we may sound like we are from the

50's era of charm school etiquette, but we're going to say it anyway. We believe that you should always try to look your best around your favorite guy. I know, some of you are saying "ugh! You mean I have to put on make-up everyday?" Yes, we think you should put some work into your appearance EVERYDAY! Of course, if you go to the gym together, well, we can always find those exceptions, but don't get so lazy that you present yourself as putting forth little effort to keep his attention. Every man loves it when their ladies are looking attractive and smelling terrific. Remember, we are talking about the first three months here, so we think you should still be dressing to impress your man. No offense ladies, but showing up in an oversized sweat suit, hair a mess, and no make-up most likely won't illicit his affections. Putting forth the effort will be rewarding!

Don't Give up all of Your Friends

The greatest life-line for women is their girlfriends. Being that women are the world's communicators mixed with the fact that we are emotional creatures by nature, unlike men, we need other women to bounce things off of. We have a tendency to over-analyze and repeat ourselves. Men are problem solvers. Once you start in on how your day was at work with the overbearing boss, men will immediately start to formulate a plan to solve the problem. Most women don't want their guy to solve the problem they just want to be heard. You may find it beneficial to also lean on your girlfriends when you "need to talk" so you're not entirely relying on the man in your life to help you work through your emotions. Truly, Jane, don't wrap your entire world around Jack because he cannot be your "everything." You will be much happier if you maintain a strong female foundation to balance out your life. One last reminder, KEEP YOUR GIRLFRIENDS!

Don't Give up Your Family, Especially, Your Own Children

We know that there are certain family obligations that we all have to tend to. If you are very family oriented, that's great, and if you have children this should be an even bigger priority. We would highly recommend that you consider being completely upfront with anyone you date about the fact that you have children, and they are a <u>Number</u> 1 priority for you. If you see that he is not being very understanding of your time with your children, we suggest you have a conversation with him as this should be a deal breaker. If you decide to introduce Jack to your children, make sure the timing is right so that the children are receptive. You don't want to introduce someone too soon. You have to be patient and so do they. Also, remember to keep some time to be shared with your children without your new beau, at least initially, so that they don't feel threatened.

NEVER give up your family for anyone. If they are the right one, they won't ask you to. Choose wisely!

Keeping Your Own Interests Intact

Jane is notorious for trying to include herself in Jack's hobbies, often at the expense of their own interests, even when they are really not into it. Sports, for example, are generally a big interest for men. While some women genuinely enjoy sporting events, there are a lot of women who don't, but participate even though their heart is not into it. We understand that you want to spend time with the new man in your life, but if you are going along only for their sake and you're really not enjoying it yourself, this could lead to some problems down the road. It's okay to say "I don't enjoy sports (or whatever)." If the two of you have other things that you both enjoy, then you shouldn't feel guilty about not participating in things that you really don't like. Having said that, we think it's important that you understand that there is give and take in a relationship so you may consider attending some of these events just because you care. Now, if you find at this point that you're running into snags with not finding much in common at all, and both of you are just going along with the other, this may be something you need to take a hard look at. Don't compromise the hobbies/activities that you enjoy for the sake of a man. You are entitled to have things you like to do so don't let go of things that bring you joy and gratification for anyone.

Listen to Your Friends

None of us ever wants to admit that our friends are right, but they are right more times than not! You should always consider the insight of your most trusted friends. Viewing the situation from the outside is always clearer than viewing it from the inside. For you Jane, emotions are the biggest blockers of reality. Those rose colored glasses can get so rosy that you can barely see out of them. Women are notorious for making excuses for bad behavior! It's vital that you see clearly at the beginning stages before you get in so deep you start to feel like you're in quick sand. A good friend will be gentle, but honest, when pointing out the reality of the situation. We highly recommend you are receptive to what they are saying. Don't take it personally because if they genuinely care about you, then they only want the best for you.

We all want Prince Charming

Prince Charming is really only in a fairytale, ladies. Instead of a knight on a white horse, you will most likely get a donkey and the ass that's riding it! All kidding aside, happiness is what you make it. No man in the world, not even our famous prince, can make you happy or complete your life. Happiness comes solely from within and no outside source can bring that to you. Many women make the mistake in thinking that when they find "Mr. Right" everything else in their life will fall into place. Here is how they think: "Oh, Michael and I are so happy. I know he is my 'everything' and he will adore me endlessly till the day I die. He will take care of me financially, emotionally, physically and is my savior." Wow, that's awfully big shoes to fill, don't you think? Talk about pressure! I think even your ass would run for the hills with his donkey right behind. Make your own happiness by having your own friends, spending time with your own family, and providing your own financial security because no one knows what tomorrow will bring. So be ready for anything and work on finding your own yellow brick road, it will make having a partnership so much more enjoyable.

> "Pop cinnamon rolls in the oven an hour before your date comes to your home as men associate the smells of vanilla and cinnamon with love!"

Don't be a Chameleon

Did you ever notice those women who you are used to seeing in jeans and a T-shirt all of sudden start wearing mini-skirts or low cut tops? You think, "Wow, have you seen how Sally has been dressing lately?" Then you find out that she has a new boyfriend who likes her to dress a little more provocatively. Being Sally's friend, you are thinking, "This really isn't Sally at all." You can tell that she doesn't even feel very comfortable in those clothes. Pleasing your boyfriend can be a good thing to a point, but losing your identity to please him is not.

Eventually, you will realize how unhappy you are being someone you are not.

Another example would be, say, you are a very social and outgoing person and you meet his family or friends and find them to be extremely conservative. You may try to suppress your own personality and end up feeling like a child in church. You will eventually resent having to feel this way and may take your frustration out on him. Now, if you like to dance on tables at parties, you could probably learn to tone that down a bit while around his family or friends, but you shouldn't have to be something you're not just to fit in. Our advice: don't change who you are!

Building and Maintaining Respect

Women love to be honored! There is nothing better than to have Jack say, "This is my beautiful, smart, fun and adorable Jane." He might even share a couple of cute and wonderful stories where you came out shining. Men, also really (secretly) want to be adored. Most men's egos are very fragile. If you build him up, you will have a man jumping through hoops of fire for you. However, if you belittle him, knock him down or embarrass him, even in a joking manner, publicly or privately, this will eventually tear the fibers of the fabric of your relationship. Treat your man with high regard and respect him for the good man (we hope) he is. Everyone likes to be appreciated. Women like compliments pertaining to our physical attributes and accomplishments. Men like compliments as well, but, complimenting on how well they do on a project or task, is even more important to them. Let us give you an example. Say your guy fixes that bathroom faucet that is leaking. Instead of saying, "Wow, that looks really nice" try saying "Wow, I can't believe that you know how to do that and so well. What an excellent job, I love it." He will beam up like Captain Kirk back to the Enterprise.

Start a Tradition between the Two of You

Most women love romance and we feel that traditions can build on the foundation of romance. We hear a lot of women complain that the romance is gone out of their relationships (side note, these are generally women who are in long-term relationships and the on-going dating has stopped). Traditions have a way of bringing you closer together. So, start something at this point (early on) that can last for many years. We have a fine example to offer you. We hear every day how our environment is being ravaged by us humans. So, each spring you and Jack can purchase a small tree and plant it either in your yard, or in an open space. Tag it with your names and a short note to each other. Then visit the trees each year and see how they are growing along with your relationship. This can serve as a measure of long term growth and the building of strength in your relationship.

Include Him in Your Life

Okay, let's get this issue of family introductions out of the way right off the bat. Every dating experience is different. We don't want you to get too caught up in the formalities of meeting the family. If you don't feel ready to introduce Jack, then don't. It's really that simple. On the other hand, if you do feel that you'd like to introduce him, be sure he's ready for that experience. If not, then please don't push it. Leave it for another time. There is nothing wrong with going to your family functions alone for a while until you both feel the time is right.

If you are a divorcee with children, the decision to introduce Jack to your children is strictly up to you! Do not let anyone push you into making that introduction until you feel ready! We would suggest that you start out in small doses with the kids. Don't all of sudden have him involved in everything you do with them. This will most likely make them feel threatened and you want your kids to be comfortable. PLEASE DON'T RUSH THIS!

Having said all of that, let's get back to the topic at hand, which is including them in your life. At some point, day-to-day living should start being shared. This is where you should start to see the real person coming out. You can feel free to include him more in your life than just a few dates. You can even start to coordinate your plans for the weekend, that kind of thing. You should also feel very comfortable at this point in hanging out together with your friends. We are not talking about living together here. We are just saying that you should be increasingly spending more time together and doing things with others in your circle.

CHAPTER 9

You've Really Got a Hold on Me

Your song is almost complete. We've helped you formulate the words, added the melody, and established the beat. Now it's time to put the music and lyrics together for your love song. Music can be magical and fill your life with hope, love and happiness. It can keep you dancing under the stars forever. Keep dreaming, keep dancing, keep creating, and keep the love inside you alive. Good music never dies nor should your love!

Determining Values for a Lasting Relationship

Not that we know anything about lasting relationships, ha ha! We can, however, share what we know about having good values. First you need to determine your values and the qualities that you have and desire in another person. So, let's assume you have done that. Now the trick is to be able to recognize them in the Jack or Jane you are interested in, without being overshadowed by a pretty face or a charming personality. Open up those eyes and look past the good looks and let's take a look at the inside. Let's face it, how many Hollywood stars do you hear that divorce the most gorgeous men or women on the planet! Perhaps they couldn't get past the looks and see that this person really doesn't share their values.

Here are some we consider to be important ones and should not be overlooked:

<u>How you were raised and how they were raised</u>

Are they similar? We don't want to say that having really different backgrounds can't work. We do feel, however, that the basis of your upbringing and the values you were taught need to be on the same page as theirs. This will avoid a lot of complications in the future.

<u>Children</u>

How important is this for you? Do you have or want children? If so, then we would recommend you find someone who enjoys children. You can validate this by asking questions or, better yet, seeing how they interact with children around them. Remember, seeing is believing! If they do not share your desire to have children, then don't be naïve and think you can change their mind. Please don't think that this is a good compromise to make. "Oh, I'll just have one to make them happy." Children are not couches that can be replaced when you decide they don't fit your lifestyle any longer. This is a very important subject! Not that it needs to be addressed on a first date, but should come up fairly quickly between you.

> **"Don't set your expectations too high as it will lead to disappointment. Just have fun!"**

Patience/Acceptance

How do they handle stressful situations and their anger? Are they prone to temper tantrums in public places? Do they lose their cool frequently over minor inconveniences? These should be deal breakers. If they are displaying this kind of behavior now, it will only get worse! Have they expressed how they handled a breakup from a prior relationship? If they are a stalker, run for the hills!

Gossip

Do they gossip about everyone? Are they excessively negative toward everyone they know and meet? These are signs that they will be a blamer and are not humble. They will most likely not apologize or take responsibility for their actions. They may even try to turn it back on you. This shows signs of an untrustworthy person. Watch yourself! Jack and Jane, this will not be an easy person to co-exist with, trust us!

Love

Does this person love on many levels? Do they display kindness and compassion toward others, even strangers? Do they have lots of friends? Do they show kindness toward animals? All of these will be tell tale signs of their heart. If they don't treat people or animals kindly, most likely they won't know how to treat you well either. Lots of people can fake love or kindness in the beginning to win you over. Over time the truth will come to be known, will you be willing to see it? Open your eyes!

Identifying Common Interests

While this subject is important, it's not as important as the values, so reference the above section as many times as you need to in order to make sure you understand it, capici? Okay, onto common interests. Everyone knows it's more fun to have someone you like, who likes you too, and enjoys the same things you do. Now, we don't mean you have to share everything. You can have different interests as long as the major ones aren't different. A major one is, Jane wants to live in the mountains and Jack wants a penthouse in New York. Unless you have unlimited funds and can afford both, WAKE UP! This is really where you need to "Get it Right, Jack . . . and Jane!"

You preferring wine while he prefers a beer is a minor difference. Let's face it, you probably don't want to crawl under a chassis and get a hair conditioning treatment by his motor oil. At the same time, he probably won't want to spend the entire day clothes shopping, right? These we can work around as long as there are other things that you enjoy together. It doesn't really matter what those common interests are, as long as you have enough to keep the two of you connected and interested in each other.

When to Become Exclusive

Obviously, this will be different for everyone. The relationship will take on its own pace. Determining when to become exclusive will be up to you and the person you're dating. One thing we want you to think about is how serious you are about this person. Be careful that one of you isn't thinking its exclusive and the other isn't. This can be a tough subject to discuss because we are now assuming that "feelings" have come into play. If you don't want to be exclusive, yet you want to continue to see this person, it's only fair that you are up front. You need to give them the opportunity to decide if that works for them. Be prepared to lose out on dating them if they can't or don't want to be with someone who is dating other people, and you're not willing to commit to dating them exclusively. We think the key here is to be honest, upfront, and respect their feelings on this issue. Becoming intimate does NOT mean that you are exclusive.

Unlike your favorite story book, not all relationships end up with you finding your prince or princess, right out of the gate. Sometimes we compromise too much of what we are looking for because we jump the gun on getting to the "relationship" part. We forget that the initial "dating" part is essential in making a sound decision on whether this person is right for you. Give it some time as a good thing is worth waiting for.

> **"Don't talk politics or religion on the first few dates, unless you enjoy conflict!"**

Role Playing

In today's day and age, many men will say that women should also contribute to the household income. This casts them in the role of being a provider as well as a nurturer. Never has there been a time like this before. Throughout history, men have been the providers and women have taken on the responsibility of being mother, wife and homemaker. Women, however, have taken on this new role with great enthusiasm and we now find that women want a partnership rather than a dictatorship! In reality, though, we are made different. Women are natural born nurturers and men are natural born hunters (providers). We think it's important to understand these differences. When these roles are totally reversed, it usually doesn't work. So as not to upset those that it is working for, we will say that a working role reversal is the exception not the rule. Most women we have talked to have told us they usually start to resent their man if they don't feel they are taking on a leadership type of role. They express that even though they are very independent women, they'd like to feel that they don't have to do it all. Now, understand that we don't feel it's necessary to have a man take care of us women in order to be happy. What we are saying is that in a relationship there has to be a balance. When you allow each of the individuals to take on the roles that come natural to them, it works much better. During the initial few months, the roles each of you will establish should come to light. Pay attention and be sure you are comfortable with the roles you each begin to assume.

Common Courtesy and Consideration

Make sure you are considering that things happen in life that you cannot always control. If, for example, you planned dinner for your date and your date is running late and you're starving, eat a snack to tide you over. Don't act like a hungry lion and bite their head off when they arrive. Now, if this is a constant issue where they set a time and are ALWAYS late, then perhaps this is something you need to discuss with them. Take a step back and consider whether this habitual behavioral problem is something you can make a concession for. Now, if they are planning a dinner and you are running late, be sure you call as soon as possible to let them know. This is common courtesy and will help you avoid major pit falls and fights. We are not talking here about 5 minutes late we are talking 20 minutes or better. Basically, treat them with consideration as you would like to be considered. Exercise patience, communication and restraint. Take 10 deep breaths before you open your big mouth or you'll regret it later.

Never stop being a Lady or a Gentleman

For you Jack, don't think that just because you've been on a few dates that you can slow down on being a gentleman. You should ALWAYS be a gentleman! No matter whether you are first dating or married 60 years. What does it take to open a door or help her with her coat? Or, how about dropping her at the door, especially, if it's raining? You guys have no idea how far this will get you. It's not what you say that impresses us, <u>it's what you do</u>. A woman will often jump through hoops of fire for men who treat her well and appreciate her! You guys always want women to act like a lady, then, act like a gentleman. The rewards will be worth it. Oh, by the way, don't put on the act only in front of your friends, women aren't dumb and it makes you look like a big old fake and they are not impressed with fakes. Be a gentleman whether it's just the two of you or out in public. If you find this too difficult and don't have a clue, rent a few Cary Grant flicks and get educated!

For you Jane, if you want your guy to be a gentleman then you need to be a lady. What do we mean by this? Don't embarrass yourself by improper behavior or foul language whether it's just the two of you or out in public. This is the time that you build and maintain respect. If you don't respect yourself, then you can't expect anyone else to respect you. We don't mean that you can't loosen up and have some fun, but let's not be lifting our tops for $0.50 plastic beads. Come on ladies, let's show a little class. If you need some help with how to class it up, read a book on charm or rent some classic movies starring Grace Kelly, Audrey Hepburn and Sofia Loren. They will teach you how to use your womanly wiles, so pay attention!

When to Get More Comfortable

Now, Jack, we don't mean loosening your belt after you've eaten too much or kicking off your shoes and putting your smelly feet on the coffee table. And, Jane, we don't mean giving yourself a pedicure in the living room while your toenail clippings sail into his cold beer. This pertains to feeling a little more comfortable about sharing your daily lives even to the extent of just hanging out with each other and not doing anything.

You can start to feel like you can have a dinner and movie night at home, having barbecues with your friends, playing board or card games, you get the picture. This does NOT mean that you give up courting. You still should be going out on dates at this point as well. Hopefully, this is the time where you get an opportunity to see a glimpse into each other's lives and how each of you deals with normal day-to-day activities. You should be getting to know each other from the inside out. If for example, you are a neat freak and they are a slob, this can be a problem down the road. Be aware of what you are seeing and know what you can live with and what you can't. Keep those rose colored glasses OFF before you get too involved emotionally.

The "I Want My Mommy or Daddy" Syndrome

Sorry, Jack, Jane is NOT your mommy, nor do they want to be! Women are not interested at this point in coming over and cleaning your house, making dinner for you and your children, and doing your personal errands. If you choose to make this a more permanent situation, then we can talk. While you are dating, though, clean your own house, cook your own food (unless we like to cook and feel gracious enough to do that for you once in a while) and do your own errands. During the first three months, you should still be finding time for yourself to accomplish these daily tasks. If you happen to get the flu, call your doctor or your mommy, don't call Jane. She doesn't want to get the flu and she doesn't want to see you yet in this condition. She'll be happy to call and see how you're doing, but don't expect her to play nursemaid. At this point you are still dating and should not consider this to be a relationship. So don't expect them to act like a wife, when they are barely a girlfriend.

Sorry, Jane, Jack is not your daddy and nor do they want to be. They are not interested in "rescuing" you from every little crisis that pops up during the day. If daddy was "money bags" to you, don't expect your guy to peel off bills at your every whim. Okay, having said that, if you happen to be lucky enough to find a guy who not only cares about you, but enjoys buying you gifts, we say enjoy the attention. But don't base your dating decision on how daddy treated you. This is an adult relationship between a man and a woman, not to be confused with the adult/child relationship. It is much more attractive to a man when you are independent enough to take care of some of your own needs. Nothing is more annoying than a high maintenance, clingy, whiner. Please don't be one!

Keeping the Fun Alive and the Romance Burning

Like the song, "Staying Alive," we think that fun and romance should stay alive throughout the entire relationship, meaning until the day you kick up the daisies. There is nothing worse than hanging out with someone who is a bore and is no fun. There is no greater feeling than sharing laughter and being a little goofy with each other to keep the fun alive. One way to really kill a new relationship is to allow it to become mundane and predictable. Romance takes work and effort, but it doesn't have to require big gestures. A simple text message or an email can do wonders in making them feel special. Men and women like to know that you are thinking of them so be spontaneous and creative. As they say, "people don't remember what you say or what you do, but they will always remember how you made them feel." Really, that is the truth! If you make them feel like there is no one else in the world, you will take their breath away.

> **"You should approach a potential Jack or Jane in places other than bars and nightclubs!"**

Don't Hang onto Someone Because You Don't want to be Alone

This is a serious topic for us because so many people do this. They hang onto relationships they know aren't going anywhere because they don't want to be alone. We can't tell you how hurtful this is! Leading someone on until you find someone better isn't right, especially, if you know they truly care about you. Don't use people as fillers in your life, it's not fair and it's not right. If you have issues with being alone, then we suggest you seek some professional help. It's not healthy to be afraid of being alone. Using people is unacceptable! If you continue to focus on "finding a man or woman", you will most likely settle for Mr. or Ms. Right Now when Mr. or Ms. Right may be just around the corner. You'll end up missing them because you've picked the fruit from the ground, instead of taking the time to climb the tree and choosing the prime fruit at the top.

Also, if you happen to believe in "karma" you may find that what you give, you get back ten fold. So, if you don't want this done to you, then we recommend you don't do it to someone else. Sorry for being so direct, but people's feelings and emotions are not yours to play with, and <u>should never be treated</u> <u>with such disregard</u>.

How to Identify That a Relationship Isn't Working

If you find that the person you are dating increasingly becomes less available or seems to be impatient with you, this could be a sign of things to come. Jane, in general, may find it hard to hurt people's feelings so they will often use more passive approaches to ending relationships. Jack, on the other hand, can sometimes be more direct. Once they decide the race is over, then, like they say in NASCAR, they "Get er done!" They flat out may just tell you they don't want to see you anymore. I know this feels like the most hurtful way to handle it, but in reality it really is the best. It's honest, forthright, and saves you a lot of guesswork, time and heartache.

A couple of tell tale signs may be (1) that you start to feel like they quickly lose interest in your conversations or (2) you find they have a wandering eye. In either case, you may want to consider initiating a conversation to see where they are at. Unfortunately, this will most likely lead to a break up. Tough to handle, we know, but better now than later. Don't take this personally, it simply means they are not the right one for you. You are now free to find the one who is right for you.

On the flipside, you may be the one that that is starting to see them in a different light. If you're finding that little things irritate you or if given the choice, hanging with your friends sounds better, then it's probably time to address the need to make the final cut. We hope that you will step up to the plate and find it in your heart to be gently honest. Doling out the truth can be painful, but if it is inevitable, why waste any more of your (or their) time than you have to?

How to Deal with Someone Who Can't Let Go

You need to be careful in this day and age as we have all heard about those stalkers! Now, without getting too deep and scaring the daylights out of you, if you have a real problem with them following you, threatening you, or losing control, you may need to get the authorities involved. Having said that, what we are talking about here, is more during the initial stages of a break up where they continue to call or email and try to convince you to take them back. We are going to ask that you allow for some sensitivity when dealing with this issue. If, though, they are dropping in on you, you may need to be more stern and direct so they understand that this is unacceptable behavior. We are assuming, of course, you were honest and direct in your break up and you're not playing games or leading them on. Most people may have a tough time initially, but after a week or so (assuming you are steadfast in the break up and not giving false hope) you should see them start to move away from you. Always use kindness as the tool in ending any relationship. Remember these words "anger only keeps you connected, forgiveness and speaking from the heart, will help you disconnect."

No, You Really can't be Friends (too soon)

As mom always says, "time heals all wounds." This is true. When emotions are raw, they need to be defused and it simply just takes time. At this point, no, you cannot be friends. Okay, really, how can you expect someone to be friends with you when they have feelings for you that transcend friendship? Use a little common sense here! Just because you don't have feelings for them, you have to recognize that they may still have feelings for you. We don't care how much they say they can just be friends, they usually can't, nor can you for that matter! There are some break ups that just have to be final, period! Others where friendship can replace dating down the road, are more rare, but not impossible. Don't expect that you will be friends with every past date. Having said that, the only instance we feel you can be friends right away is when the break up is amicable or if there really wasn't a connection for either of you there in the first place.

Recovery

If you were really hurt by a recent break up, don't jump into another one to soothe away the pain. Again, not fair to the other person. Be honest with yourself about whether you are emotionally available to date again. No one can tell you when you feel ready, so take all the time you need. Of course, if this was a fairly short lived dating experience (a month or two) you should be pretty much ready to be back in the game rather quickly.

Grieving is a way the body purges negative feelings, so don't underestimate the power of a good cry. As long as you don't let your sadness get out of control and linger too long so that depression starts to set in. If you are feeling like you're having trouble moving on, seek some help, especially if it's over a short-term relationship. A good tool to use during this time is to treat yourself to something you really enjoy. Do things that make you feel good about yourself like getting lost in a good book, eat chocolate (seriously), and take time to spend with your friends and family. Indulge in all of the things that make you feel better. Why not get a new haircut. As Angela would say, "If you can't change your life, change your hair."

"Don't overlook the value of love letters!"

Friends of Your Ex's are off Limits

Ask yourself this question, "Is dating your ex's friend really worth ruining a friendship over?" How would you feel if your ex decided to date one of your friends? This is what we are talking about here. Sometimes, you have to look past your own selfish needs and see the bigger picture. For you Jack, beware that most girls believe it to be a cardinal rule that they don't date each other's ex-boyfriends.

If you do find yourself attracted to one of your ex's friends, do the right thing and talk to your ex. If they really want to date you, any good friend will clear it with their pal first. You may be surprised to find that they are fine with it, but if they aren't, then make sure you know the score before you dive into a shallow pool. You just might break your neck!

How to Get Through Minor Bumps in the Road

Patience, patience, patience! Learning how to control your anger is a difficult task. Once you're in the middle of an argument or disagreement, it's tough to pull back and exercise self-control. Of course, anyone will tell you to try to diffuse the situation before it detonates, and we think this is great advice. The trick is not to blow things way out of proportion. As the old saying goes "don't make a mountain out of a mole hill." Arguing is never the answer! It only causes stress and resentment. If you find that you are at odds over some issue, talk it out. If you feel that they are getting irritated or you start feeling that way, it is best to walk away and discuss it later. A word of warning, if you have a person who doesn't seem to be able to control their temper, this is a big red flag, especially, if you are seeing this in the first three months. It only gets worse! We think at this stage in a relationship, if you are having big disagreements, you may want to consider whether this is something you want to continue.

Moving on Down the Road

Success is arriving to a place of happiness and contentment through some effort. We hope this book has been a road map that was easy to follow. Perhaps you have successfully recognized the red flags. In which case, you are now traveling down the road in a different direction that will lead you to the right Jack or Jane for you. Maybe, you have successfully initiated the beginning of a beautiful relationship. Even if you are married, we hope this has encouraged you to continue dating to keep the love alive. In any case, we hope we have instilled in you some of our wisdom, and that you will be successful in finding the right person, if you haven't found them already.

As there is much more road for you to travel, we will continue to provide you with future maps on our website that will ultimately lead you to your destination.

For information about us and how we can further help you, visit our website!

CHAPTER 10

Creating a Winning Romantic Dinner (Even you can't mess it up!)

Setting the Mood

What you will need:

Table Cloth
Cloth Napkins
Wine and Water Glasses
Candles
Centerpiece
Motown Music (a must!)

If you do not have the above items and you are on a budget, you can find most of them at a good dollar store near your home.

Try to purchase matching linens if at all possible (e.g., table cloth and napkins). Put the table cloth on your table, along with the folded napkins. Place silverware as follows: forks on the left and knives and spoons on the right. If you are going to serve at the table, then have your plates already set. If you are serving wine, then have a wine glass along with a water glass set on the table as well.

Place your centerpiece in the middle of the table. Centerpieces can be as simple as the candles themselves or a small flower arrangement or both. If you are so inclined, you can place candles around other parts of the kitchen/living room for additional mood lighting.

Play your favorite classic Motown music in the background.

<u>Baby Love Breaded Chicken</u>

3 Chicken breasts (cut horizontally into two thin breasts)

2 Eggs (beaten in a bowl)

1 Cup of Flour (in a bowl)

1 Cup of Bread Crumbs (in a bowl)

1 Lemon (cut in 4 wedges)

2 Tablespoons of Vegetable Oil

Directions: Coat chicken breasts in Flour, then dip in beaten eggs, then coat in bread crumbs.

Heat Vegetable Oil in skillet on medium heat. Cook the breaded chicken in skillet for about 5 - 7 minutes on each side - flipping over occasionally until both sides are golden brown. Squeeze a little fresh lemon over chicken, and serve.

Going to a Go-Go Green Beans

Grab 3 handfuls of fresh green beans at the store and put in a bag. Cut the stems off and rinse.

4 tablespoons of sliced almonds

1 Package of Good Seasons Dressing, with glass mixing bottle included (prepare as box says)

Directions: In sauce pan, put rinsed green beans with 1 cup of water. Bring to a boil then turn down to simmer with the lid on sauce pan. Cook for about 10 minutes (be sure to check periodically to make sure that the water doesn't evaporate while cooking). Test with a fork to see they are tender. Then drain them and sprinkle with almonds in a dish and toss in some Good Seasons dressing to lightly coat. Salt and pepper to taste and serve warm.

Signed, Sealed, Delivered Salad

1 medium bowl of mixed greens or Romaine lettuce (washed and cut up)

1 red bell pepper (washed and sliced thin)

1 cucumber (washed and sliced thin)

1 tomato (washed and diced)

½ of a can of black olives (rinsed and sliced)

Optional: Add your favorite cheese (we suggest Provolone, cut into chunks, about 1 cup)

Use remaining dressing from Green Beans for your salad dressing or any other salad dressing you desire.

Directions: Combine all ingredients into a salad bowl except the dressing. Toss and then lightly coat the salad with the dressing of your choice.

<u>Do You Love Me Dessert</u>

1 - Pound cake (purchase at the grocery store)

1 - Quart of strawberries (cut off green stems and rinse). Slice in thirds.

1 - Container of whipped cream (like Reddi Whip or Cool Whip)

Directions: Slice a couple of pieces of the pound cake and put on two plates, cover with strawberries, top it off with whipped cream.

Made in the USA
Charleston, SC
01 November 2010